TOLKIEN'S GEDLING

1914

For Angela

THE BIRTH OF A LEGEND

Andrew H. Morton and John Hayes

BREWIN BOOKS

First published by
Brewin Books Ltd, 56 Alcester Road,
Studley, Warwickshire B80 7LG in 2008
www.brewinbooks.com

ISBN: 978-1-85858-423-2

A Cataloguing in Publication Record
for this title is available from the British Library.

Typeset in Baskerville
Printed in Great Britain by
The Alden Press

CONTENTS

ACKNOWLEDGMENTS

We are deeply indebted to Jennifer Paxman (née Brookes-Smith) for her permission to publish material from Colin Brookes-Smith's two unpublished memoirs. Her personal memories of Jane Neave and her account of the Brookes-Smith family history have been invaluable. We would also like to thank Dorothy Ritchie for pointing us the way to the *Ladies Who Farmed in Gedling 1913–1923* memoir and providing us with very useful photographic material from her own personal collection. Discussions with Birmingham historian Maggie Burns have helped us locate Jane Neave within the Suffield family background. Maggie's research into the Suffield family background has been extensive; I am most grateful for the material she has shared with me, which eventually will provide a deep and original insight into Tolkien's family background. Wayne Hammond and Christina Scull have been generous with their help, advice and encouragement throughout this project. Their generous comments on and corrections of my manuscript are really more than a writer like me, embarking on this area for the first time, might expect or deserve. Any errors that might remain in this book will be there despite their best efforts to keep me on the straight and narrow. Simon Stacey first pointed out to us the Gedling link, so we have him to thank (or to blame) for the whole project. We would also like to acknowledge the help of all the archives mentioned at the end of the book, but particularly to Rachel Hart at St Andrews, Philippa Bassett at Birmingham University and Alison Wheatley at the King Edwards Foundation, who went out of their way to provide us with very useful material. Also thanks to Mrs Thomas of

Gilfachreda for her information on Wern Villa and Miss Marian Collins for her Dormston memories.

Although this book has been written by me, John Hayes shares the authorship in so far as his research on Phoenix Farm in various Nottingham archives forms much of the factual basis of *Tolkien's Gedling*. Without his 57 pages of closely packed research, we would have got nowhere at all. This fact accounts for my drifting between the first person singular and plural pronouns from time to time.

Many of the Phoenix Farm photographs are family snapshots, often copies of copies of photographs taken on a Box Brownie. Their authorship is uncertain, but the author would be glad to acknowledge authorship in any subsequent edition.

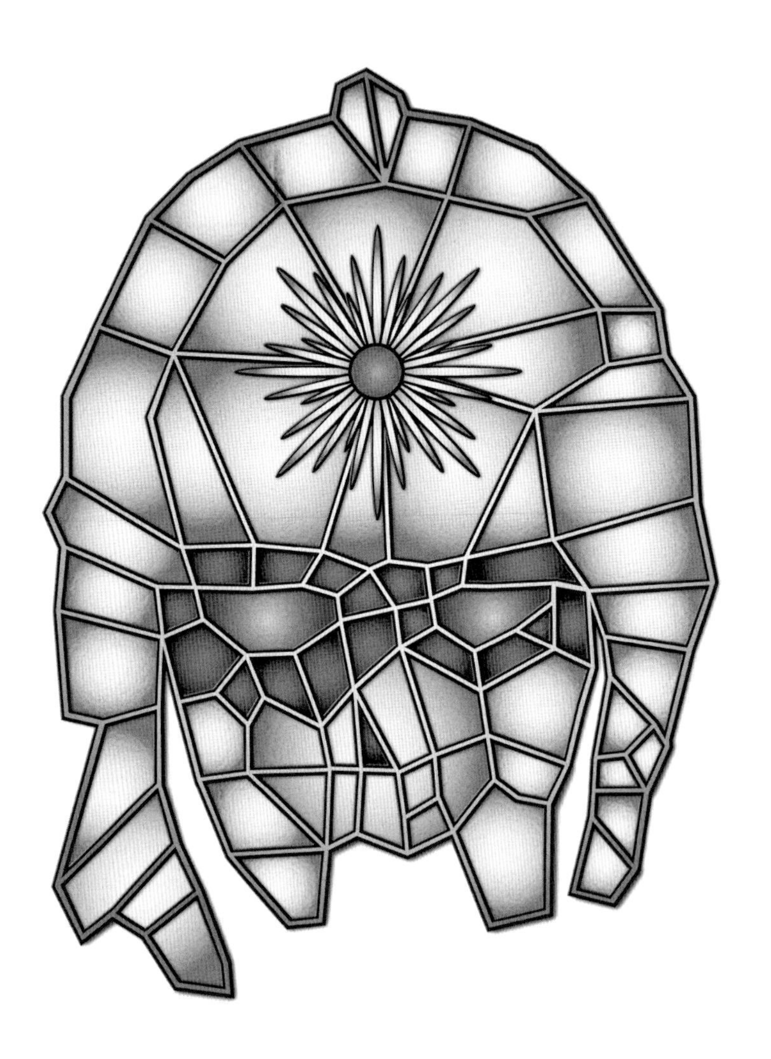

Chapter One

IN SEARCH OF PHOENIX FARM, JANE NEAVE AND EÄRENDEL

When I first heard of the Gedling Tolkien connection, it was at a reading of his poems given at the literary society at my son's school, which just happens to be Tolkien's old school. The speaker was somewhat disparaging about the Nottingham suburb in which I was born and I felt an irrepressible urge to vindicate the place. This was partly from a sense of loyalty, but partly because I was curious about Gedling a hundred years ago and what J.R.R. Tolkien was doing there. My subsequent quest has led me into interesting territory and I'm glad I took up the challenge.

I remember Gedling fifty years ago, when it was on the verge of the expansion that led to the building of the Coal Board estate and the subsequent in filling of much of the land on the south west side of Arnold Lane. I have clear memories of the excavation of the land which used to be Phoenix Farm, where my father and I pretended to be Hilary and Tenzing, clambering over the heaps of earth. It could be reached via a footpath that led from the top of Thorsby Avenue, where I lived, to a stile at the top of Besecar Avenue. The old wooden stile has been replaced by a more sophisticated metal affair, but the footpath is still there.

If you went in the other direction, turning right, the path, now a made-up road, led to "Donkey Hill", a steep path which was effectively a continuation of Lascelles Avenue. At the bottom of Donkey Hill there was a wild and overgrown orchard and beyond that the "cow fields" which you had to cross to get to Arnold Lane. Beyond were the monumental slag heaps of Gedling colliery, which smoked by day and glowed a dull red by night.

That area, Donkey Hill, the wood and the fields, was the sort of territory children were still free to explore fifty years ago. It still holds some of my most vivid childhood memories. In preparing this book, it struck me that J.R.R. Tolkien himself was notably susceptible to childhood nostalgia, transforming his precious semi-rural years at Sarehole, near Birmingham, into a "land of lost content". I'm not sure how far you could describe life in Gedling fifty years ago as evoking "blue remembered hills" – more like grey remembered slag heaps – but we certainly used our imagination on those few acres, concocting all kinds of mythology out of very ordinary material. It was from unspectacular places like Sarehole and Gedling that Tolkien's Shire [1] was constructed.

The wood was haunted by some fearful entities which took the form of "the pellet gun gang" and "the catapult gang". We never actually saw these famous hooligans, but we accepted their existence with a sort of religious certainty. They were manifestations of our primal fears, no doubt. We knew every corner of the wood and curiously, a very Tolkienian touch, named two of the trees "the mother tree" and "the father tree". Or perhaps we named them – this may have been a local tradition. The wood was alive for us and embodied mystical personal presences. Down near the hedge which bordered on the cow fields someone had dug a large hole in the clayey soil, which led to a sort of passageway. We could actually see where the hole came to an end; nevertheless, it was rumoured that this work of unknown excavators was really a back entrance to Gedling pit. It must have been some kind of Freudian fascination that imbued this unimpressive hole with a deeper significance. Somebody must have owned this land, but we never saw any evidence of it. But the cow fields, which were reached via a large gap in the hawthorn hedge, were meadows belonging to a farm, and now I know that that farm was once known as Phoenix Farm.

In his memoir of Gedling, which forms the basis of my chapter on Phoenix Farm, Colin Brookes-Smith remembers being thrilled by the

---

[1] The Shire is home to Hobbits in *The Hobbit* and *The Lord of the Rings*, the place from which both adventures start out and to which they eventually return. Recognizable elements of Sarehole, then a Worcestershire village but now engulfed in Birmingham, where Tolkien spent the happiest years of his childhood, as well as Dormston, where Jane Neave lived for twenty five years, are present in Tolkien's maps and illustrations.

sound of the pit cages accelerating up and down. Even now I remember clearly lying in bed and listening to the familiar sound of the winding gear and the railway shunting going on around the colliery. In childhood, we make stories out of ordinary things, and this process is exactly the one that fuelled the writing of J.R.R. Tolkien throughout his life. His imaginary land was somewhere else, but my lost Gedling is still vivid in my mind all these years on.

Although much of this has changed over the last half century, there are still things about the landscape that impress me. For a start, there is that stunning view over the Trent valley that I had from my bedroom window in Thorsby Avenue. It was rumoured that on a clear day you could see Belvoir Castle. And I shouldn't omit that pungent yet somehow homely aroma wafting over from Stoke Bardolph sewage works when the wind was in the east. I remember also the way the poplar trees punctuated the hillsides with their characteristic upright and elegant shapes. Those things are still there. Some things have improved – the slag heaps have now been grassed over, and the little stream that once formed the boundary of Manor Farm runs a little cleaner than I remember it.

One important aspect of Tolkien's Catholic belief was the doctrine of original sin, and if his work avoids direct Christian allegory, it is infused with a strong elegiac feeling about lost innocence and the destructive power of greed. This, combined with the gloomier elements of the Anglo Saxon mentality, create a poignant sense of ultimate defeat in his writing. At the end of *The Lord of the Rings* and *The Hobbit* the ancient order is restored in The Shire, but in the real world Tolkien undeniably felt a sense of loss about places like Sarehole and, perhaps, Gedling, where in his youth he found a temporary model of an England unspoilt by progress.

* * * * *

It was a surprising discovery that J.R.R. Tolkien had written a very significant poem at his Aunt Jane's Phoenix Farm in Gedling: if Tolkien is particularly associated with any part of the country, it is with the West Midlands, and particularly Worcestershire, the ancestral home of his maternal Suffield family. There is no evidence to suggest that Tolkien in any way incorporated this Nottingham suburb (then village) into his fictional landscapes, but it is certain that Phoenix Farm saw the birth of his mythology in the form of the poem he wrote there on September 24th 1914.

The Voyage of Eärendel the Evening Star is the first of his poems in which the figure of Eärendel appears, and Eärendel goes on to enjoy an illustrious future in Tolkien's subsequent writing, a crucial character in *The Silmarillion* and an important element in the mythical background of *The Lord of the Rings*. Most of the major biographies of Tolkien make mention of this, devoting a sentence or two to the episode. It interested me for two reasons: first of all, Gedling was where I was born and spent my early childhood, and I still have connections with the place; secondly, I picked up a suggestion that Tolkien's Gedling poem was written at a sort of crossroads in his life where the twenty two year old writer started to find his true direction. Creative breakthroughs often occur at a time of personal crisis, which was certainly what J.R.R. Tolkien was experiencing in September 1914. In fact, a sense of deep dislocation and loss during the whole of WW1 led to his first significant burst of creativity, when he started to explore the mythical material which later fed through into *The Hobbit* and *The Lord of the Rings*. It was in retreat from the horrors of war and in recuperation from a lingering dose of trench fever that Tolkien conceived these very first outlines of his mythology, now to be found in the two volumes published as *The Book of Lost Tales*.

Intrigued, I started to look for any material on Phoenix Farm and the shadowy figure of Jane Neave, but found very little, so I asked my friend John Hayes, who still lives in Nottingham, to see if he could come up with anything. Shortly before Christmas 2006, John walked into the customary Wednesday social gathering at All Hallows Church Gedling. Talking to the friendly natives, John was able to take the first steps in establishing the location of Phoenix Farm. He was also told, rather surprisingly, that in the churchyard lay the grave of Edwin Neave, Jane's husband, and the date on the grave (1909) suggested that Jane Neave was in Gedling at a much earlier date than we, or anyone for that matter, had previously imagined.

Trusting initially to the kind of primary data that can be found in electoral registers and trade directories, we began to establish more about the Neaves and the extraordinary Phoenix Farm project over which she presided between 1912 and 1922.

It also began to appear that the period around 1911 was an interesting one in the history of Gedling and recourse to The Manvers Collection in the Nottingham University Archives showed that substantial land sales had taken place which involved Phoenix Farm. And delving into hitherto unknown archive material on Jane Neave showed that she too was experiencing a significant upheaval in her life around this time.

In this process, especially concerning Jane Neave, we began to realise that we were making discoveries that called for small but significant changes in and additions to the standard Tolkien biography. It was interesting to see how single-minded research using public records could subvert the assumptions made by biographers whose main recourse was to letters and other secondary material. This was partly down to archive material that is now available in digitized form, which previous researchers did not have access to; on the other hand most of the really important material to emerge still came from dusty written records which John Hayes meticulously explored in traditional archives. Having chosen to research a fairly narrow period in detail, we found that we were unearthing a few original pieces of the Tolkien background. Consequently, we began to feel that the material that makes up this book would not only be of local interest, but would present Tolkien scholars with some new factually based material.

One such discovery concerns the name Phoenix Farm, which Jane Neave changed from Church Farm [2] sometime in early 1912. The fact that Jane had changed the name had meant that initially the farm was difficult to locate, showing on maps and other documents as either Church Farm or Dairy Farm. "Phoenix" is now a familiar name in the area, in the form of an avenue, a pub, a Methodist church, a used car dealership and a drop-in police-station, and I suppose no one gives it much thought. With the benefit of hindsight, however, it is clear that "Phoenix" is quite an unusual name for a farm in an area where farms are normally named after local features or people. Jane had a habit of changing names, and when she later started farming in Worcestershire, she changed the name of her farm there back to the ancient name of "Bag End", a name which will be familiar to all

[2] The farm is listed as "Church Farm" in Gerring's *History of Gedling*.

Tolkien enthusiasts as the home of Bilbo Baggins in *The Hobbit* and of Frodo in *The Lord of the Rings*.

In researching this book, we have been blessed to find a number of individuals who have helped us locate some rich source material. We have Dorothy Ritchie to thank for supplying us with a copy of *Ladies who farmed in Gedling 1913–1923*, a photographic memoir, written by Colin Brookes-Smith in 1979 about his life on the farm during WW1. And looking for permission to quote from this material led us to his daughter, Jennifer Paxman, who has been unstintingly generous in furnishing us with other photographic material and first-hand recollections of Jane Neave. This sort of good will, added to the helpfulness of archives around the country, has been invaluable. We have been lucky, but this luck rides always on the generosity and interest of others.

Our discoveries about the Brookes-Smiths and the help of their descendants have been crucial to our project. We have been able to establish more than was known before about this family, in partnership with whom Jane farmed at Gedling during the WW1 period. In addition, the material with which Jennifer Paxman has been able to furnish us, combined with some discoveries of the indefatigable Suffield historian Maggie Burns, has opened up some insights into their relationship with J.R.R. Tolkien and his maternal family, the Suffields, of whom Jane Neave was one notable member. I am confident in claiming that the photographic material concerning Phoenix Farm as well as other pictures of Jane Neave, Jane's farm at Bag End, John Suffield and one picture of the Swiss holiday party are published here for the first time.

Because Colin Brookes-Smith's memoir *Some Reminiscences of J.R.R. Tolkien* includes a detailed account of Tolkien's 1911 Swiss holiday, which is interesting *per se* as a reflection on episodes in *The Hobbit* and *The Lord of the Rings*, we decided it was appropriate to include it here. This holiday was in many ways a curtain raiser to the Phoenix Farm era, initiating a period of contact with Jane Neave and the Brookes-Smiths.

Even at its inception, this book was forking off in different directions, for as soon as we started to establish something about Phoenix Farm, we found other related material that seemed interesting. The fact that J.R.R. Tolkien wrote his very significant poem at Phoenix Farm is a major curiosity, and probably mainly coincidental, although we have allowed ourselves to speculate a little about possible links between the place and the poem. There is material here concerning the transformation of rural into suburban England, which was one of Tolkien's later preoccupations, as well as the encroachment of industry in the form of Gedling Colliery. However, it is impossible to say whether Tolkien at this early stage in his career was aware of or moved by the changes that were taking place in Gedling. There may be more to discover in the mounds of so far unpublished correspondence that lies jealously guarded in various Tolkien archives. On the other hand, we are confident that this book not only does what it set out to do – namely to reconstruct Phoenix Farm – but also contains material that adds in minor but interesting ways to our knowledge of Tolkien.

The chapter entitled "Gedling for Sale", the fruit of John's research in the Manvers archive, will be mainly of interest to local people; we started looking into this material in search of information on Phoenix Farm and Jane Neave, but it seemed to have some intrinsic local historical interest. As far as Tolkien studies are concerned, I freely confess to my amateur status compared with others who have dedicated years of their life to a study of the author and his work and have bowed in all cases to advice given from more knowledgeable quarters. Nevertheless, it may be that my neutral approach, which tries to be fair to Tolkien without being too reverential, has something to recommend it. But for those who wish to be clear about the Tolkien related material in this book, I offer the following pointers:

- The Phoenix Farm chapter offers a little previously unpublished anecdotal material about J.R.R. Tolkien at the farm, based on Colin Brookes-Smith's memoir.

- In establishing more about Jane Neave than has previously been published, I clear up at least one little mystery about Tolkien in 1904 and suggest ways in which Jane Neave was influential in the author's life. My speculation about Jane Neave as a possible prototype for Gandalf adds some new evidence for this well-known but possibly fanciful theory. Tolkien and his wizards constitute a massive area of study, and I confine myself to certain unexplored character traits in Jane which have emerged in researching this book.

- The chapter on the Gedling Poem gathers together material on the biographical context and the provenance of Eärendel in Tolkien's later body of work. Other critics have been here before, but for the purposes of this book, I have tried to take a fresh run at it, claiming no great originality.

- My consideration of the name Eärendel makes a thorough examination of Tolkien's probable sources while arguing for some reassessment of the author's much later account of his discovery of the name.

- Finally, the bonus chapter on the Swiss holiday of 1911 gives a more detailed account of this episode, I believe, than has been written before and makes a useful comparison with Tolkien's own account.

Chapter Two

"DEAREST AUNT JANE"

This was the way in which J.R.R. Tolkien addressed his letters to his maternal aunt, Jane Neave. She was certainly a figure of some importance in his life and in a letter of 1961,[1] written two years before her death, he counts himself blessed to have such a shrewd and sound-hearted maiden aunt.

The quest that sent us in search of Phoenix Farm and the Gedling poem led us first of all to Jane Neave, who owned the farm between 1911 and 1922, or co-owned the farm as it turned out. We had no idea that this investigation would turn up so much new and interesting material about Jane and Gedling, or that we would be dealing with such an impressive woman. This new material rests firmly on the foundation of documentary research, but we are deeply indebted to Jennifer Paxman, the daughter of Colin Brookes-Smith, for additional insights into Jane as a living personality without which this brief account would be much poorer. These memories go back to the 1930s and 1940s when she and her sister Julian visited Jane at Dormston. They consist of vivid snapshots of a handful of significant incidents and general observations of character but they also are based on family lore concerning Jane, which, considering the close relationship of Colin Brookes-Smith's family with Jane over a period of fifty years, deserve to be considered reliable.

Emily Jane Neave, née Suffield, was Mabel's, Tolkien's mother's, younger sister by a couple of years. By nature she was modern, independent and progressive in her attitudes. Like Tolkien, she pursued her academic interests with dedication and determination following a

[1] *Letters*, p.308/9.

strong family tradition of artistic, technical and literary interests. Mabel Tolkien's educational background is a complete mystery but she was competent in languages and had considerable artistic skills, both of which she was able to pass on to her son, kindling a life-long interest in linguistics. Jane, who appears to have received a more formal education, was more inclined to the sciences and it was she who taught the young J.R.R. Tolkien geometry in preparation for his entry examination for King Edward's School. The death of his widowed mother Mabel in 1904 from diabetes, then an untreatable condition, was understandably traumatic to the twelve-year old Tolkien. He felt the premature death of his mother acutely and he may have found in his mother's younger sister something of the maternal stability that he craved. For although Jane was childless herself, she had strong motherly instincts which extended not only to her orphaned nephews but to friends of the family like the Brookes-Smith children. In a conscious choice of role, she signed her letters to May and Colin Brookes-Smith "M/A" standing for "mother/aunt".

It is difficult to judge the extent to which Tolkien was in contact with Jane over the seventy years of their acquaintance, but she was always at least a background presence, and he visited her at various locations throughout his life, in Scotland, in Gedling, at her farm in Dormston, and at his brother Hilary's fruit farm near Evesham, in Worcestershire. She was also there during his childhood and the traumatic period of his mother's death. In the letter alluded to at the beginning of this chapter, it seems that the rock-like firmness of her physical and mental constitution evinced a long lasting admiration from her nephew. He continued to correspond with her to the end of her life, when she was ninety and he was seventy. Touchingly, these letters show no sign of condescension on Tolkien's part. Jane at this age was still intellectually capable and her observations are capable of evincing detailed and thoughtful responses from her nephew. In his letters, she is addressed "Dearest Aunt Jane", a term of endearment that tells us something about the relationship.

Tolkien would have been first aware of Jane when, at the age of three in 1895, he returned with his mother from Bloemfontein to his mother's family home in Ashfield Road, Kings Heath, in Birmingham. The visit turned out to be a permanent one when his father, Arthur Tolkien,[2] died in South Africa in early 1896, leaving Mabel to pick up the pieces of her life with her two sons in Birmingham. At this time, Jane was a schoolmistress in Birmingham and living at home but engaged, or shortly to be engaged, to the lodger, Edwin Neave. Although it seems that the Suffield family were fond of Edwin, there was something about him that did not match up to their social aspirations. Edwin had a good education and was making his way in the world of insurance, but the Suffields were of some local standing [3] in Birmingham, fairly prosperous and highly literate, and it may be that Edwin did not seem such a good catch for the talented Jane. Mabel, Tolkien's mother, had faced similar disapproval from her father when she was courted by Arthur Tolkien and one may speculate that there is something of a jealous or over-protective father syndrome at work here. Significantly, perhaps, Jane had played go-between during the courtship of Mabel and Arthur, clandestinely delivering notes between the two, and this interest she took in her sister's love-life may account for the subsequent lasting interest she took in her nephews, Hilary and Ronald.

The Suffield family, with whom Tolkien identified more strongly than his Tolkien relatives, were a large Birmingham clan well known for their industry and enterprise. Local historian Maggie Burns has done much to dispel the possibly misleading impression given of John Suffield in Humphrey Carpenter's biography of Tolkien, which finds him trudging the streets of Birmingham "cajoling orders" for Jeyes Fluid.[4] Although he had his ups and downs in the business world, the family was mainly prosperous and by the early 1890s, John had an iron foundry [5] in Birmingham as well as his Jeyes Fluid franchise.[6] The Cotton Lane house, which was his permanent address after Ashfield Road, shows a clear increase in prosperity. John, who lived until the age of 97, dying in

[2] Despite the exotic name, Arthur Tolkien was a native of Birmingham. This account does not deal with Tolkien's paternal family partly because Jane Neave was a Suffield and partly because J.R.R. Tolkien always identified strongly with his maternal family.

[3] I am indebted to the research of Maggie Burns on the Suffield family.

[4] *Biography*, p.26.

[5] Birmingham University Archives. Jane, at Mason College in 1892 gives "iron founder" as her father's profession. This initially puzzling entry has been confirmed by the researches of Maggie Burns who has discovered a likely location of the foundry.

[6] Jeyes themselves have no record of John Suffield's activities, but, as has been pointed out to me by Birmingham historian Maggie Burns, this brand of disinfectant was at the time a much vaunted new product and association with it may not have implied being down-at-heel.

1930, was something of a local celebrity, well known for his travels, his active interest in literary matters and debating societies as well as his preaching. It may be that his down-to-earth Unitarian beliefs disposed him well to take an interest in the education of his daughters and he was willing to pay substantial fees for Jane's secondary education. (Emily) Jane was a Suffield through and through, sharing, as Tolkien did, John Suffield's artistic talent [7] and his interest in poetry,[8] although her interests were primarily scientific.

Jane must have excelled at her school, the prestigious King Edward's High School for Girls,[9] and went on to teach at the King Edward's Foundation Bath Row School in 1892 at the age of twenty. Her service there was continuous, with one leave of absence for illness in 1903, until 1905, when, at the age of thirty-three, she offered the governors her resignation in order to get married to Edwin Neave. This 1903 leave of absence for illness is somewhat mysterious and may have more to do with the onset of her sister Mabel's illness. It may have been a trying time for the family when all hands were needed on deck. (Jane was not beyond some innocent subterfuges of this nature, as we will see later with reference to her reasons for a later resignation.) Nevertheless, her teaching record shows that she was a highly competent and dedicated science teacher, who took an interest in sports (tennis is mentioned) and earned an extra five pounds a year for taking "school drill responsibilities". On leaving, she was thanked for her "unselfish work in superintending its affairs". Before she left Bath Row, her interest in education led her to stand for and be elected to the Birmingham School Board in 1901 and a photograph [10] of her at this time shows a severe and impressive looking young woman in her academic robes.

Remarkably, during this full time employment, she registered on a science degree [11] course at Birmingham's Mason College, the forerunner of Birmingham University. Between 1892 and 1895, she followed courses in

---

[7] Maggie Burns has unearthed a delightful little watercolour by Jane Neave featuring children sitting on a farm gate apparently being told a story by an adult female figure. It shows some artistic skill and features a sunflower, Jane's favourite flower.

[8] Maggie Burns has uncovered evidence of John Suffield's talent for drawing and also an irrepressible tendency to write doggerel, which perhaps, he passed on to his famous grandson!

[9] Information in this paragraph taken from King Edwards Foundation Archives.

[10] Thanks to Maggie Burns for this discovery.

[11] Information in this paragraph taken from Birmingham University Archives.

botany, geology and physiology and was awarded her BSc in 1895. (She had to take leave of absence from teaching to sit her final examinations.) In fact, after graduation, she continued to attend lectures in physiology and also attended a series of popular lectures entitled "Britain", which perhaps indicates that her interests ranged more widely than the simply scientific. As Tolkien points out at the beginning of this chapter, Jane's science degree was a remarkable achievement; we may speculate that it also laid the foundation for her future career as farmer. In the late Victorian period, especially in a city like Birmingham with its progressive non-conformist ethos, this kind of educational opportunity was opening up for women, and Emily Jane Suffield was just the kind of woman to take advantage. A few years later, the new Birmingham University was proud of its women graduates and early motion pictures [12] exist of their graduation processions.

These details of Jane Neave's achievements help to fill out a previously sketchy outline of her academic career. It is worth noting that her teaching and pastoral career lasted over twenty years, and that after she turned to farming, she kept up her connections and interest in the world of education through her friends Dorothy Le Couteur and Helen Preston. Apart from J.R.R. Tolkien, she was the only Suffield to hold a university degree, making her in one way his intellectual peer, but it would be wrong to underestimate the degree of literacy and general intellectual interest in the Suffield family, which were an inspiration to her and her nephew.

The fact that Jane was teaching in Birmingham until 1905 finally helps to clear up a little mystery concerning Tolkien's stay in Hove during his mother's final illness in 1904. The assumption, made in Humphrey Carpenter's biography and followed by others, had been that Jane and Edwin were married and living in Hove when Tolkien was dispatched there to be out of the way. In fact he was sent to stay with his "uncle" Edwin who was then working as an insurance agent in Hove, and Tolkien's much discussed postcard [13] entitled "They Slept in Beauty Side by Side", if it is of anybody, shows himself and his uncle sharing a double bed. It would have been unthinkable for the twelve year old Tolkien to send his family a postcard representing the unmarried Jane and Edwin in bed together.

---

[12] The remarkable BBC series *The Lost World of Mitchell and Kenyon* showed one such graduation procession.

[13] *J.R.R. Tolkien Artist and Illustrator* p.10.

Similarly unthinkable in today's climate, would be the idea of the boy and his aunt's fiancé sharing a bed, but in those days people were not so finicky about sleeping arrangements. And of course, it is also possible that this picture is the twelve-year-old Tolkien's idea of a joke and they never shared a bed at all. But the fact that Tolkien was sent to stay with Edwin Neave at all suggests the degree of trust the Suffields were prepared to put in him, despite what might have been their other reservations.

Jane Suffield and Edwin Neave, her fiancé of many years, were, in fact, married in Manchester in the summer of 1905.[14] Edwin Neave's family were Salford based so that would explain the location, but it was and is normal for a young woman to be married from her father's house. The presence of her older brother Roland in Manchester at this time [15] may also contribute to explaining the location of the wedding. Perhaps, and this is speculation, John Suffield still thought that Jane was throwing herself away on Edwin. She was certainly ending her teaching career by getting married. Until the mid-century women teachers were expected to give up their careers when they married.

Edwin Neave, perhaps, deserves a few words here, particularly as it is his career that first finds the couple moving to Gedling in 1905. In Humphrey Carpenter's biography, Edwin Neave appears at Ashfield Road in the mid 90s as "the sandy haired insurance clerk".[16] Carpenter informs us that John Suffield did not approve of him, thinking him "common". Neave was the son of a Salford pawnbroker, and may have sported a northern accent. He was an accomplished amateur banjo player and, the banjo being a remarkably loud instrument, this may have been a source of understandable annoyance to John Suffield as well as anyone else within a hundred yard radius. (He was a gifted entertainer and Maggie Burns has uncovered evidence of him performing in local amateur concert parties in the 1890s.) However, while working in Birmingham, Edwin was an insurance *inspector*, not a *clerk*. It's a small but important distinction, as inspector implies a degree of formal education and a greater measure of responsibility. When he moved to the Hove offices of the Guardian Fire

---

[14] The crucial discovery of this date was first published by Maggie Burns in *Amon Hen* September 2006. Maggie was first in the field with this discovery, although different aspects of the 1904/1905 period were discovered independently from different sources by the two of us.

[15] Discovery of Maggie Burns.

[16] *J.R.R. Tolkien: a Biography*, p.26.

Insurance Company in 1902,[17] it was for a promotion to "agent". In 1905, he was promoted finally to "Resident Secretary" of the Nottingham branch of the Guardian Assurance Company,[18] a title that means he was in overall charge of the branch. His death certificate gives him as "Manager of an insurance company".

We now know that Edwin's career had finally put him in a position, at the age of thirty-four, to support a wife. In 1905, the couple moved to a house called The Cottage,[19] which stood in Shearing Hill near the station, and stayed there till Edwin's death in 1909. Gedling would have been an excellent and logical choice. Edwin had a commuter railway station a few yards from his front door, but the area was still semi-rural as well as being cheaper than the more fashionable suburbs of Nottingham. Edwin is listed as having "land and tenements" in the 1909 electoral register and maps of the time clearly show that the odd dwelling houses on the railway side of Shearing Hill had enough land attached for modest horticultural activities. One is tempted to think that while Edwin was at the office, Jane might have been trying her hand at growing things. We know very little about the domestic life of Jane and Edwin during this period, but we do know that Edwin took out a subscription for Charles Gerring's weighty *A History of the Parish of Gedling* in 1908, and this indicates that they took a serious interest in their new home and perhaps intended to stay.

This first period of residence in Gedling was cut short by Edwin Neave's death from bronchial pneumonia at the age of 37, on May 8th 1909. His grave can be seen in the picturesque graveyard of All Hallows Church. Probate of Edwin's will was granted 14th June 1909 and he left his wife £730.16s.4d.[20] This sum, which might have bought Jane a couple of cottages at that date, gave her some financial security in the short term at least. It may also have given her the collateral that allowed her to bid for Church Farm (Phoenix Farm) two years later.

There is a suggestion that married life for Jane and Edwin Neave was not entirely happy. In later life Jane always referred to Edwin as "the man I married"[21] rather than "my husband". The couple remained childless, and it

[17] Information provided by the Brighton History Centre.

[18] *Wright's Directory* 1905 p.285.

[19] The Cottage almost certainly stood to the left of the station as viewed from Shearing Hill, on the site now occupied by 1960s houses.

[20] Nottingham Archives: wills going to probate 1909.

[21] Jennifer Paxman reporting her father.

has to be said that it is somewhat mysterious how the independent and career-orientated Jane came to be a housewife. Colin Brookes-Smith, who knew Jane from 1911 to the end of her life, thought that Edwin had a drink problem and this would certainly have caused tension between him and Jane. If the Suffields thought him frivolous, this may have been one legitimate reason. They were by no means a dour and puritanical family, but their serious-minded Christian background might have put them at odds with Edwin. Social drinking is an occupational hazard of the insurance business, or at least was at that time, and it is not unreasonable to imagine Edwin paving the way to business deals in the famous pubs of Nottingham. His cause of death is given on his death certificate as "broncho pneumonia" (sic), but whether this was down to a cold he couldn't shake off, or the final symptom of dipsomania and liver failure, as Colin thought, is a mystery that may never be solved. Whatever his faults may have been, the young J.R.R. Tolkien found in him an entertaining uncle with whom he could share a common enthusiasm for music hall songs and a certain masculine camaraderie.

With the death of Edwin, Jane was now free to pursue a career again. She was not the kind of person to remain idle and this time she moved into the sphere of higher education.

In the preparation of this book we have been lucky to unearth previously unknown details about Jane Neave's career in Scotland.[22] After Edwin's death, between July 1909 and June 1911, she was Warden of University Hall at the University of St Andrews, an appointment that caused some controversy when Principal Sir James Donaldson threatened to resign in protest. However, his doubts about Jane's suitability, which seem to have been governed largely by prejudice, were overruled by the committee and Jane, as usual, proved an exemplary employee. She seems to have been an able administrator dealing with accommodation, new building projects and "garden and grounds realignment". When she could not be persuaded to withdraw her resignation in 1911, she was highly praised by the institution who commented on "the way she has superintended and watched over the women students resident in the hall and Overflow houses, and the valuable assistance she has given in connection with the extension of the Hall buildings and the management of the institution". Many years later, her obituary in the Alumnus Chronicle

[22] Information in this paragraph courtesy of the Special Collections Department, University of St Andrew.

was even more gushing. She is praised for her "wise and gentle wardenship"; she completed the architect's design of the new wing with "antique furniture and delightful colour schemes"; particularly interesting is the following comment: "Her vivid mental life knew no boundaries, her knowledge of English Literature was so vast that one felt she should have been a professor, perhaps of poetry, a scholar and the author of many books. But she loved her own subject best and followed with intense interest its philosophy and new developments all through her life. To her friends, Jane Neave gave richly of her wisdom, her understanding and sympathy and her encouragement, but for herself asked for nothing. Her only desire was to serve others, her only anxiety lest she should ever give anyone else even a little trouble".

Given the fact that Jane was only at St Andrews for two years, this document is evidence of the profound impression Jane could make on people and the lasting memory she left behind. Admittedly, as an obituary it is likely to be a little fulsome, but it also serves to indicate the range of Jane Neave's intellectual interests, her organizational abilities, her warm humanity but also her sensitivity to the aesthetic side of things. We know that it was she who much later encouraged her nephew to publish a new and affordable version of some of his poems, but this new information about Jane's literary leanings suggests that in 1914 she was perfectly capable of enjoying an informed discussion about poetry with her nephew. When she sold Bag End in 1931, the elaborate sales brochure she prepared included snippets of Brooke and Tennyson – fairly conventional pastoral stuff, but confirming at least her fondness for poetry. A book of Chaucer and Spenser's poetry shows that she borrowed at least one book from her older brother John [23] which she did not return. The Suffield family was steeped in literature and it goes back a long way: another book in Jane's possession when she died was a copy of Sterne's *Sentimental Journey* beautifully inscribed "Sam Suffield, Bengworth, 1786".

In an unpublished memoir, Colin Brookes-Smith states that it was during her stay in St Andrews that Jane came into contact with his sisters, Doris and Phyllis.[24] This proved to be a very significant meeting, as Jane

[23] Inscribed "J. Suffield Jr. 1877" in a carefully crafted gothic script.

[24] "At that time my two sisters, Doris and Phyllis were at St Catharine's School in St Andrews Fife.... I am not sure of this, but I think it must have been in St Andrews that my mother first met Mrs Edwin Neave, the Tolkien brothers' aunt". CBS.

subsequently formed a strong friendship with the girls' parents, Ellen and James Hector Brookes-Smith. Jane and Ellen seem to have instantly recognised fellow feeling. They were both strong minded women and within a year, they were contemplating a very major project together, namely the joint farming venture in Gedling.

Jane gave as reason for her resignation from University Hall her mother's illness, but we now know that she had other plans. Doubtless, her mother's illness was genuine, but in March 1911, a Nottingham estate agent called Holroyd had bought Phoenix Farm (then Church Farm) on her behalf. It is possible that her resignation actually depended more on the success of her bid for the farm rather than her mother's health but this is speculation only in the absence of clear evidence. Her address on the later deeds of transfer is still given as University Hall, St Andrews. Indeed, it may well be that St Andrews was her place of residence until April 1912 when she had vacant possession of Church Farm for the first time.

It seems a reasonable assumption that Jane's scientific interests in botany, physiology and geology, as well as the land and buildings management role she had developed in St Andrews, led her to try her hand at farming. One might have guessed this, but in the memoir by Colin Brookes-Smith to which we make extensive reference in the chapter on Phoenix Farm, Colin explicitly states that Jane has always fancied trying her hand at agriculture. She had the driving force and skills to organise such a project and her knowledge of the well kept Gedling farm would have suggested this as a likely spot. Her change of career from an academic to an agricultural one was certainly a bold move and typical of her single-minded personality. Women farmers were not entirely uncommon in this era; it was a role often adopted by widows and daughters of farming folk. Jane was unusual in as much as she came from an entirely different kind of background and a different career.

In the summer of 1911, with the purchase of the farms complete, Jane, along with Ronald and Hilary Tolkien, accompanied the Brookes-Smiths and an odd assortment of other friends on a walking tour of Switzerland. It became a significant episode for Tolkien and Jane Neave, and is referred back to in various ways in both their lives. Jane held on to the alpenstock and cloak she wore on this holiday and returned at least once on a botanical holiday later in her life. Tolkien used one particularly hair-raising episode from the 1911 holiday in his later fiction, and the final chapter in this book is devoted to Switzerland.

The holiday over, Jane, the Brookes-Smith family and Hilary Tolkien were ready to get down to the serious business of taking over the running of their farms in Gedling.

A full account of life at the farm is given in the Phoenix Farm chapter.

After the Phoenix Farm partnership was dissolved in 1922/23, Jane continued to farm but in Dormston in Worcestershire. Dormston stands on a hilltop in an altogether more spectacular landscape than Gedling, in the rolling countryside between Stratford on Avon and Worcester. Quintessentially English, the nearest village is Inkberrow of *Archers* fame. To the west, there is a view of the distant Malvern Hills, hardly mountains, but constantly "misty" in a suitably Tolkienian way, characteristically bluish purple from a distance. Tolkien and his maternal Suffield family were proud of their Worcestershire roots, and in his visits to Dormston, he must have felt, as Jane did, a sense of coming home. This sense of belonging was certainly promoted by John Suffield,[25] who rightly took pride in his family background. The Suffields were well known in the West Midlands and, to illustrate this fact, John Suffield liked to boast that one day a postal package addressed simply to "Mr Suffield, England" found its way to the right address.[26]

For several years, Jane put her practical knowledge of agriculture to work at Dormston Manor Farm, a rambling brick and half-timbered building dating from Elizabethan times. She found that the local and ancient name of the farm had been "Bag End", a name which Tolkien adopted in his writing of *The Hobbit*. There has been a great deal of speculation about the name "Bag End" and although the name must have had a certain resonance for Tolkien to adopt it into his fiction, its origin is simple and as stated above. Unlike the poetic and mythical Phoenix, this time there is something earthy and self-deprecating about the name; it is common-sense, homely and unpretentious. Although it is indeed in a cul-

---

[25] One branch of the Suffields lived in Bengworth near Evesham in the 18th century, but there are other connections with Coventry in Warwickshire. Maggie Burns has shown that the Suffield connection with Worcestershire is not exclusive.

[26] This story from Jennifer Paxman as part of Brookes-Smith family lore.

de-sac, situated at the end of a track leading back from the village at an acute angle, many farms are cul-de-sacs one way or another and the correspondence between the French and English versions of "cul-de-sac" are almost certainly coincidental.[27]

Throughout the twenties, Bag End, like Phoenix Farm, was a place of regular conviviality, including among its guests, the Tolkien brothers and their wives, Colin and May Brookes-Smith and, in their infancy, their daughters, Julian and Jennifer. In his last years, John Suffield was a regular visitor at Bag End, although his permanent residence was in Cotton Lane in Moseley. Bag End was brick built at the front and half-timbered at the back, a house of considerable size that could easily accommodate several visitors. The farmhouse consists of three substantial wings; it mainly dates from the late sixteenth century with elaborate over mantles and staircases of that period, but one of the dovecotes is inscribed with a date of the early fifteenth century and probably some structure had been there since the Saxon period.[28]

During the 1920s, Jane, who seemed to favour all-women enterprises, had another farming partnership with Marjorie Suffield, née Atlee, who had been a land girl on Phoenix Farm, but this partnership was dissolved in 1927 when Marjorie married Jane's nephew, Frank. In 1931, Jane, then approaching sixty, gave up the Bag End Farm but retained both of the small farm cottages belonging to Bag End, one, Church Cottage, for herself, while the other at the far end of the lane, Orchard Cottage, she let out to a tenant. It is likely that the severe agricultural depression that hit Worcestershire in the 1930s may have contributed to her decision to give up farming.[29] Her earlier career at Phoenix Farm saw a market boosted by the demands of the war, but as the twenties progressed the outlook for farming was distinctly dismal, only to pick up again during WW2.

---

[27] Although the intriguing "Bag Inn" appears on a 1731 map of Dormston, along with a thumbnail sketch, this is almost certainly a clerical error. In any case, Bag End is a most unlikely location for an inn. Most likely the Bag element is a personal name from the Saxon period, and Bag End means something like "The boundary of Bacga's land". But in his "English Place Names" Eilart Ekwall points out that the "bacga" root may well refer to some kind of animal rather than a personal name as it is never combined with the word for a settlement, rather a landscape feature.

[28] Dormston is mentioned in The Doomsday Book as "Deormodealdtun". So it was "eald" or "old" even then.

[29] The Worcestershire Records Office have very full records of this difficult time.

The early thirties were an unsettled time, finding Jane living briefly with the Brookes-Smiths in Chislehurst in Kent, and then for a couple of years in Chelmsford.[30] Her stay at Chelmsford was part of a religious quest, her object being to be close to the religious retreats run by Evelyn Underhill at the Essex Diocesan House. Now an almost forgotten name, Evelyn Underhill achieved fame in the twenties and thirties by writing about the restorative nature of "shutting the door" on the world to achieve mystical union with Christ. As with Jane, her academic achievements were notable, and she was the first woman ever to be invited to give a series of lectures at Oxford University. Her mentor was the equally famous and controversial Catholic theologian Baron von Hugel. These were people whose deep religious convictions seem to have overridden the confines of sectarianism divisions in a kind of mystical ecumenism. Jane and Evelyn both had roots in the West Midlands, and although I have not been able to establish a relationship between the two, I think it is certain that the two women met during her stay in Essex. Although an Anglican, Jane's was a form of religion that easily merged with some aspects of Catholicism. She donated the Madonna and Child relief still to be seen at St Nicholas' Church, which perhaps suggests something about the importance to her of the archetypal mother-child relationship. Its iconic content and bold colours stand out in the otherwise undecorated church, suggesting that her religious sympathies were distinctly High Church then and that she had come a long way from her non-conformist Suffield background. But Jane's religious sensibility, like her nephew's, was not over-pious. Jennifer Paxman remembers her wearing her Austrian Loden cloak in a grown-up game of charades called Rhubarb. As she enacted the prophet Elijah ascending into heaven, she rose up from the sofa waving a stick and declaiming "Rhubarb".

Jane was a deeply religious person, so deeply religious in a mystical way that she rarely spoke of it openly except, perhaps, to May Brookes-Smith, the wife of Colin.[31] In an incident, dating to 1946, Jennifer requested to hear Elgar's Enigma Variations in a radio concert, but Jane refused, making it clear that this kind of music was not in keeping with

---

[30] Maggie Burns has established from King Edwards Foundation records that Jane lived in Chelmsford for two to three years in the early 30s. Both of us presume that this was to be near the Pleshey retreat, although that organisation is singularly unforthcoming with information.

[31] According to Jennifer Paxman.

her religious sensibilities. (Perhaps, after her Chelmsford period, she preferred the more austere strains of Hildegard.) In Dormston and Gedling, she was a regular church-goer, and the part of her that was sociably inclined would have enjoyed the community aspect of church life. On the other hand, her faith was informed by mystical Christian figures like the Abbess Hildegard of Bingen,[32] Mechtild of Magdeburg and the mystic Julian of Norwich (after whom Julian Brookes-Smith was named.) It seems significant that Jane was devoted to these three women, and although "feminist" may be an unnecessary anachronism, it is clear that she was constitutionally inclined to explore and push back the limits of women's capabilities. Her early academic career and achievements and her later ventures into farming, as well as her religious predilections are all evidence of this. It is all part of what characterises her "stern and independent spirit".

After Chelmsford, she lived for a short time in Rottingdean with her generous brother-in-law, Walter Inceldon and his talented artist daughter Marjorie (alias Wink and Mink.) She finally returned to the Dormston cottage in 1936/7 and stayed there till 1948.

The cottage in Dormston, just up the lane from St Nicholas' Church, was a simple two bedroomed affair with one living room and kitchen downstairs. There was no mains water or electricity and the lavatory was down the garden. Washing took place in the sink and baths in a tin bath. The Brookes-Smith daughters visited and took part in "Grannyish activities" like mushrooming and country walks and Jennifer Paxman remembers Jane talking about the constellation Orion as they walked home after a talk at the village hall. Jane was known as "Granny" to Julian and Jennifer, a natural extension of the close relationship that existed with the Brookes-Smith family.[33] Jennifer observes that this motherly trait was strong in the childless Jane, although she was never "cuddly". She was capable of taking a stern view of matters concerning domestic order, perhaps reasonable in a small cottage with limited space and only rudimentary facilities.

---

[32] Hildegard of Bingen, polymath abbess of the 12th century, is the first named composer in the Western musical tradition.

[33] In these more formal days, relationships between close family friends were often defined in this way, perhaps to find an acceptable from of address. To Jennifer, Jane Neave was "Granny" and J.R.R. Tolkien was known as "Uncle Ronald". To Colin and May Brookes-Smith, Jane termed herself "aunt" and signed herself "M/A" for "mother/aunt".

Back in Dormston, she became the president of the Kington and Dormston Women's Institute and, here again, Jane was the right person to fill that leading and organising role: one of the conditions for the building of the village hall was the foundation of some kind of "women's club" and Jane helped fulfil that condition. True to form, she organised several educational talks as part of the curriculum, although no doubt combining these with the less intellectually demanding activities of that august institution. Some older inhabitants of Dormston still have memories of Jane and her little Ford car, industriously earning her reputation as a well respected member of the community.

Jennifer Paxman's reminiscences of Jane Neave are vivid and telling. She was "not a cuddly type of person but endlessly interesting and unchanging". She was "tall and spare and decided and could be very funny, although not in a giggly sort of way". Indeed the few pictures we have of her suggest a strong physical presence and an imposing personality. Perhaps it was the image of Jane on a remembered Swiss holiday, and the letter 4th November 1961 in which Tolkien describes the party, that started the Jane-as-Gandalf speculation. It is an interesting idea, but one that Tolkien nowhere makes explicit. Of course, if he had this connection in mind, it would have been unthinkable for him to embarrass his elderly and revered aunt with such a revelation. But the absence of evidence can never be proof of anything and the theory has to remain questionable. On the other hand the profile of Jane that has emerged during research for this book suggests a personality which was bold and original, capable of inspiring an unusual degree of admiration. Throughout her life, Jane seems to have made an impression on people who knew her, not only her nephew, but her employers, her farming partners and even today the older inhabitants of Dormston who have memories of her.[34] Jane lived in the real world, and her religious convictions, which she lived rather than intellectualized, were strong and intensely personal. She was confident and self-possessed, feeling no need to flaunt her intellectual powers or her spirituality. To Tolkien, whose attitudes towards the opposite sex were conservative, Jane would have presented a model that defied conventional gender boundaries and it is conceivable that elements of her personality

[34] I have recently interviewed some members of the congregation of St Nicholas in Dormston who are generally aware of Jane's Tolkien connection, but are more impressed by the role Jane assumed in the community.

that he admired might emerge in a male fictional character. This is as far as the speculation can safely go. Tolkien knew Jane for the best part of seventy years but contact was probably not continuous: in 1937, her constant moves meant that he had to ask his brother for her current address so that he could send her a copy of *The Hobbit*.[35] But despite the inevitable periods when they drifted apart, Jane continued to take a solicitous interest in her nephew's late flowering literary career, marvelling to the teenage Jennifer Brookes-Smith at Church Cottage how he managed to get so much writing done with such a lively and demanding domestic life. Here perhaps, we see the elderly Jane, who liked everything "just so" in her domestic arrangements, failing to appreciate the importance of this family setting for Tolkien the writer and Tolkien the man.

After Dormston, and another short period in Rottingdean, she moved in 1953 to the fruit farm that Hilary Tolkien ran near Evesham, where she lived in a caravan, taking only a few prized possessions. But the picture of her standing in the door way of her caravan shows her in her eighties still tall and straight as a ramrod. Her final years were spent at Wern Villa in the idyllic village of Gilfachreda near New Quay in West Wales, cared for by her nephew Frank Suffield [36] and his wife Marjorie, who had a small-holding there. In 1961, it was a request from her for a "small book with Tom Bombadil at the heart of it" [37] that eventually led to the publication of *The Adventures of Tom Bombadil and Other Verses from the Red Book* in November 1962.

She died on February 22nd 1963 in Aberaeron Cottage Hospital at the age of ninety, and one may speculate that the atrocious winter of 1962/3 had some hand in this. There seems to have been a late flurry of correspondence between Jane and her nephew around this time and a long and complex letter [38] from Tolkien written in the previous year shows that she was still totally in command of her intellectual faculties until the end. Colin Brookes-Smith was the executor of her will but also named as "residuary legatee" and many of Jane's odds and ends, including some letters, went to his daughter Jennifer, who had a special interest in Jane and things to do with "Uncle Ronald". Jane is buried in the church yard

---

[35] Christina Scull and Wayne Hammond – *J.R.R. Tolkien: Reader's Guide, Chronology*, p.201.

[36] Son of Jane's older brother Roland.

[37] *Letters*, p.308.

[38] *Letters*, p.315.

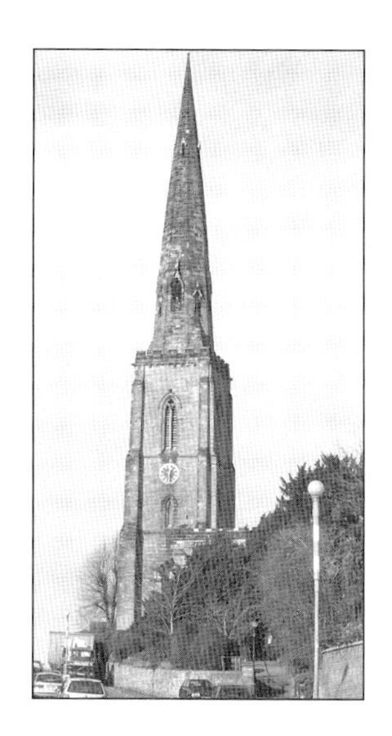

Left: The famous tapering spire of All Hallows church as seen today. Right: Gedling Colliery in 1910 shows the mine in surroundings which are still fairly rural.

The Dovecote at Phoenix Farm. The bull was also kept downstairs. On the left the covered crew yard.

Left: The Brookes-Smith sisters, Doris and Phyllis, feeding geese on Manor Farm. The first flock of geese made a V-line for the Trent, but were recaptured and their wings clipped. Right: The mannish figure of Ellen Brookes-Smith riding home after a day in the potato field with land girl Marjorie Atlee guiding the cart.

Left: Ellen Brookes-Smith in Manor Farm home field. Left centre can be seen the road crossing the railway line. Ellen's masculine appearance perhaps says something about the role she had adopted. According to her granddaughter she was "not the motherly type". Right: Seasonal labour was hired at various times on the farms – here to hoe and single crops.

Ellen Brookes-Smith. Her family thought she looked rather like Spencer Tracey.

Lowdham, Lambley, Orston (including Thoroton), Screveton, Cropwell Butler, Gedling, and Carlton,

NOTTINGHAMSHIRE.

Particulars, Plans, & Conditions of Sale

OF VERY VALUABLE

Freehold Estates

Belonging to the Right Honourable The Earl Manvers,

Comprising **1579 ACRES** or thereabouts, divided into Lots, including the following well-known Farms:—

Grove House (Lowdham), 137 a.	Marlock House (Lowdham), 254 a.
Manor (Orston), 152 a.	The Rookery (Cropwell Butler), 153 a.
Podder (Gedling), 155 a.	Dairy Farm (Gedling), 59 a.
Marshall Hill (Carlton), 115 a.	Small Holdings.

Accommodation Lands, Capital Dwelling-houses, Cottages, Garden Allotments, and Building Sites.

Which will be offered for Sale by Auction by

Messrs. J. H. BRADWELL & SONS

AT THE

GEORGE HOTEL, NOTTINGHAM,

ON

Wednesday & Thursday, 8th & 9th March, 1911,

At **2.30 o'clock in the Afternoon each day,** in the following or such other Lots as may be determined upon at the time of Sale, and subject to the Conditions of Sale herein contained.

FIRST DAY'S SALE	- - -	Lots 1 to 31B.
SECOND DAY'S SALE	- - -	Lots 32 to 82.

FOR PERMISSION TO VIEW APPLY TO THE RESPECTIVE TENANTS.

An advertisement from the Nottingham Guardian for the auctions of March 1911. In this sample, Phoenix Farm is "Dairy Farm" and the Manor Farm listed is, in fact, not the one in Gedling.

Left: Jane Neave and her Irish terrier Mona, taken at Phoenix Farm.
Right: Colin Brookes-Smith bagging potatoes, probably around 1920.
The girl in the background is Marjorie Atlee.

Doris Brookes-Smith with a cow and its bull calf. Only interesting for the view of the church and the farm buildings in the background.

Left: Land girl Margaret Goodman and Jane Neave in working clothes and characteristic head scarf. In the background can be seen the roofed-in crew yard (left) and the farm's outbuilding (right). Right: Ernest Smith and Marjorie Atlee harrowing. All the work on the farm was horse-powered until 1920 when a tractor was bought thanks to a tax rebate.

Land girls Margaret Goodman and Marjorie Atlee riding ponies in Arnold Lane. On the left can be seen the stack yard of Phoenix Farm and you can just make out Manor Farm House in the distance.

The flower and vegetable garden, which Hilary Tolkien tended at the rear of Phoenix Farm. From a similar angle, J.R.R. Tolkien made his line drawing, the only previously known image of the house. The figure on the left is probably Jane Neave.

Phoenix Farm House from Arnold Lane. It was an eccentric building, showing distinct similarities to Manor Farm House, which still stands. The wing on the right was a later addition comprising a dairy and a bedroom upstairs. One can see how Jane was attracted to this building, as she was later to the even grander Bag End.

Land girl Marjorie Atlee with a Sussex wagon laden with bags of potatoes. Marjorie, who appears on many Phoenix photographs, went on to farm with Jane at Bag End and married Jane's nephew Frank Suffield at Dormston in 1927.

Nearly all of the work on the farm was non-mechanised, but every year a steam-driven threshing machine was hired in, here seen in the "stack yard" behind the roofed crew yard.

Left: Waggoner and ploughman Ernest Smith, a Leicestershire man, who lived in the tied cottage on the Manor Farm side of the road. He was paid the generous wage of £5 per week and was the only permanent employee. Right: Apple picking in the orchard. From left to right, Colin Brookes-Smith, his sister Phyllis, Mrs Neave and Doris Brookes-Smith assisted by geese, hens and dogs. The face of Hilary Tolkien can just be made out in the tree.

Left: James Hector Brookes-Smith with another dog, the Pekinese, Golly who liked to chase sheep. James Hector was never a farmer, but a gifted amateur engineer who "literally kept the wheels turning on the farm". Right: James Brookes, retired clergyman and Ellen Brookes-Smith's older brother, working at his prize vegetables in the garden of Manor Farm House.

of St Ina's chapel, which stands adjacent to the elegant manor house of Plas Llanina. It is an atmospheric place and her simple headstone, much plainer than most of the surrounding monuments, commands a view of the sea.

When she died, Jane had already divested herself of many material possessions,[39] but her life achievement is to be measured in terms of the deep affection in which she was held by those who knew her and her example as an adventurous and independent spirit. If she had continued her academic career, it is possible she might have achieved more in the way of celebrity, but her career choice of farmer, which began at Phoenix Farm in 1911, petered out in the depression of the 1930s. But without Phoenix Farm and later, Bag End, certain aspects of her nephew's fictional world would have been different, and, who knows, even non-existent, for the Gedling Eärendel poem was the start of it all. For the determined researcher, there is almost certainly more to add to the account I give here, but as far as I know, it is the most detailed account of her life so far, a life that reminds us how many unsung yet remarkable ordinary people lie in the shadow of the famous.

[39] Although she did leave about £6000, a fair amount of money. This detail, a matter of public record, perhaps sheds some light on the £100 gift from her nephew that Jane declined. She was fairly comfortably off, although J.R.R.T. may not have realised this.

Chapter Three

GEDLING FOR SALE, 1910–1911

The Ordnance Survey map of 1900 shows Gedling to be still very much a village. There is a little cluster of new buildings in the angle between Westdale Road (now Lane) and Main Road and some new dwellings in the area bounded by Main Road, Tennyson Avenue and Waverley Avenue, but apart from that, the houses, cottages and farms are scattered between fields, allotments and orchards. There were also "osier beds" for basket and fence making, and the name "willow" lives on in various guises in the area. Its close proximity to the populous city of Nottingham and its rich soil made it an ideal location for market gardening. The only modern intrusion on the area is the railway line, which came to Gedling in the 1880s. By 1911, the year of the great Gedling auction, things have changed somewhat and Gedling is beginning to be a true suburb of Nottingham. New building has appeared along the side of Main Road and Tennyson Avenue has become the pattern for development between Main Road and Burton Road. The presence of the commuter railway and the pressure of population are beginning to make their mark and the keen eye of the developer would have spotted Gedling as a prime site for suburban expansion, but still, at this time, Gedling retained much of the character of a rural village. White's Directory for several years around this time has Gedling as "a pretty and improving village" and it is true that the suburban development, such as it was, was of a fairly pleasant character aimed at the Nottingham trades people and professionals. Gedling Colliery had not gone through the rapid expansion of deep mining that started in the 1930s, eventually resulting in a massive and spectacular slag-heap to the north of Arnold Lane. A picture of the colliery in 1910 shows it still surrounded by fields, although its presence and that of the colliers would have made it a typically Nottinghamshire blend of industry and agriculture.

When J.R.R. Tolkien visited his brother Hilary and his Aunt Jane at Phoenix Farm, as he did in 1913, 1914 and 1915/1916,[1] he would have found it a fairly congenial place. He might even have compared it favourably with the Warwickshire village of Sarehole where the happiest years of his childhood were spent. Skirting industrial and suburban Nottingham on the train, he would have found the short distance from the station in Shearing Hill to his aunt's farm an essentially rural walk. With his growing knowledge of Old English, he may have thought about the rich mixture of Anglo Saxon, Norse and even old Celtic names (the rivers and streams) in which the area abounds as well as the name Gedling itself, after the Germanic chieftain Gedla, who followed the Ouse from the Trent and founded the village in this fertile spot. Then there was Arnold, in Old English "Ernehale" the "haunt of eagles", which may also have captured his imagination. The poem he was to write in 1914, *The Voyage of Eärendel the Evening Star,* was steeped in a mythical Germanic pre-history.

The magnificent church of All Hallows with its elegant and daringly designed spire[2] would also have been a point of interest. Jane Neave, who took an interest in churches wherever she lived, is sure to have shown him round and talked about the long history of the place. On this or his previous visit, he would have seen his uncle Edwin's grave in the churchyard nestling among the monuments of famous Nottinghamshire cricketers.[3] He probably knew something of the recent social revolution that had changed the place forever and allowed his aunt to buy Phoenix Farm.

You only have to look at the names of streets and pubs around the Gedling area to see the ghostly remains of an older aristocratic pattern of land ownership in the area: Cavendish, Chesterfield, Portland, Manvers, Thorsby, Lascelles, Pierrepont, Welbeck are the kind of names that crop up

---

1 *The J.R.R. Tolkien Companion and Guide* – Christina Scull and Wayne Hammond – for these dates. There is some uncertainty about the last one.

2 There is a remarkable degree of "entasis" – the degree to which the spire is tapered, in this case 2ft.

3 Alfred Shore (who bowled the first ever ball in Test Cricket) and Arthur Shrewsbury.

again and again. Until 1911, nearly all the land between Westdale Lane and Arnold Lane was owned by Charles William Sydney Pierrepont, Fourth Earl of Manvers and this chapter will be concerned with the process whereby these holdings were auctioned off in the spring of 1911. It is a story which directly concerns Jane Neave, as she and Ellen Brookes-Smith bought a considerable chunk of Gedling in the form of Phoenix Farm and Manor Farm at this time. And tracing the letters and other documents held by The Manvers Collection in Nottingham University Manuscripts, we can get some insight into the radical social changes that were happening immediately prior to WW1.

It was Chancellor of the Exchequer Lloyd George's Finance Act of 1909, commonly known at "The People's Budget" which lay at the root of these changes. The act, which imposed a range of new taxes on the wealthier classes (probably 250,000 people), had a famously rocky ride before it obtained the royal assent, a ride which saw the House of Commons seriously at odds with the House of Lords before the issue was finally resolved in the Parliament Act of 1911. It is arguably the most radical piece of social legislation of the 20th century, paving the way for the later Welfare State. The increased tax burden on individuals like Lord Manvers meant that they had to sell off large swathes of property, and although they did not go down without a fight, as we shall see, the writing was on the wall by the summer of 1910 when the following article appeared in The Times [4], 9th August 1910:

> "Tenants on farms belonging to Lord Manvers at Gedling, Lowdham, Mapperly and Carlton, Notts have this week received notice to quit owing to the proposed sale of the estates following upon the increased burdens imposed by the Budget.
>
> Much of the land is adjacent to a populous mining district and within easy reach of Nottingham. It has increased considerably in value during the last 20 years and in the near future will be required for building purposes. The estates comprise about 300 acres.
>
> Lord Manvers has given the tenants the first chance to purchase, agreeing to two thirds of the purchase money remaining on mortgage at four per cent."

---

[4] The Times, August 9th 1910, page 11 column 4. Nottinghamshire county Library on microfilm.

On the same day, a similar but longer article appeared in the Nottingham Guardian [5] which was strongly sympathetic to the land-owning interests and attacked the radical policies of Lloyd George. It saw no benefit in breaking up the large estates and looked for alternative ways of broadening land ownership with different kinds of taxes, the kind of ideas that the House of Lords were stalling with at the time.

This unscheduled announcement, inaccurate in small but significant ways, caused considerable consternation to Lord Manvers' capable land agent, R.W. Wordsworth who, in a flurry of letters [6] comparable to the swiftness of the email today, asks "by whose authority" this article was published. It is a telling phrase, as authority in all its forms was a keystone of the ancient regime of which he was a part. Over the next few days, Wordsworth bitterly complained to The Times about the article, never quite stating what he was objecting to, but clearly discomfited by the letting of the cat out of the bag. In fact, his main problem was over the phrase "notice to quit"; none of the tenants had received notice to quit and in truth this would have been the responsibility of prospective purchasers. Neither had it been decided at this point which properties were to be sold. Lord Manvers himself, currently resident at Aviemore and looking forward to the grouse shooting season, showed himself fairly indifferent. He must have been something of a nightmare for the conscientious Wordsworth to deal with [7]:

"Dear Wordsworth,

I am sorry you had all the unsigned cheques of mine returned to you.

I hope these sales will go off well when the time comes.

You will probably have seen the paragraph in The Times of Tuesday headed "Lord Manvers' estates". Hot summers weather here now and traipsing the moors tomorrow will be warm work for those engaged in it.

Yours faithfully

Manvers"

---

[5] Nottingham Guardian August 10th 1910 page 6, Nottinghamshire Country library microfilm.

[6] Manvers Collection, Nottingham University Manuscripts, ref MA 2C 164 page 392A.

[7] Manvers Collection, ref. MA 2C 2/118 1&2.

Poor old Wordsworth battled on manfully against the newspaper editors until the 16th of August when Manvers shrugs off the whole business, saying that the damage had been done and could not be undone.[8] In the end, Wordsworth had to concede that the article was substantially correct, but it had caused him some embarrassment.

Land Agents like R.W. Wordsworth played a crucial role in the social organisation of Britain at the beginning of the century. He was a devoted servant of the old conservative landed class but the conscientiousness with which he discharged his duties, his wide knowledge of land management and the sheer scope of his responsibilities are in some ways impressive. With only two assistants at his Thorsby Office, he effectively managed estates amounting to 38,000 acres[9] and all the human problems that arose with many hundreds of tenants, most of whom he probably knew by name if not by face. We estimate that in a typical year, Wordsworth dealt with about 8,000 pieces of correspondence alone concerning such things as accounts, sales, housing, policing, and pension for retired employees. He was deeply conservative in his attitudes, showing unquestioning loyalty to Lord Manvers, but he did his best within his own terms of reference.

An example of the kind of insecurity the rumours of forthcoming land sales in Gedling was causing may be illustrated by the case of William Armstrong.[10] Writing to Manvers' estate office at Holme Pierrepont in July 1910, Armstrong, a sub-postmaster living on Arnold Road (now Arnold Lane) wants to be given first option of purchasing his property.[11] He wants an interview to discuss this, but the office replies that it has not yet been decided which tenanted properties will be up for sale, so he had better wait and see. Armstrong however, in a rather desperate letter, informs the office that he is thinking of improving his building and cannot go ahead until he has a reassurance that he will be allowed to continue in his home. Again, he is stalled by the office, and in the end bundles up all the letters and sends them off to the highest authority, R.W. Wordsworth. Wordsworth replies to the same effect. Happily for Armstrong, he was able to buy his home (Lot 62) when it came up for auction, scraping the money together with the help

---

[8] Manvers Collection, ref. MA 2C 164 p.402.

[9] The Complete Peerage Vol. 8 (Nottinghamshire Archives).

[10] Manvers Collection, ref. MA 2C 19/40/ 1–5.

[11] The post office can be seen on the map of Phoenix and Manor Farms, a little way up Arnold Lane on the same side as Phoenix Farm.

of the sub postmistress, Clara Smithurst [12] and her colliery blacksmith husband, Harry Smithurst.

The Manvers Collection contains many more letters from tenants who are acutely insecure about the land sales. Typical is this extract from a letter [13] from T.E. Pickin of Fledborough near Newark:

> "Dear Sir,
>
> I have heard several rumours that Earl Manvers is going to sell his property at Fledborough, which I most sincerely hope is not true if it is can I have the offer of the farm I am occupying I hope his lordship will not forget we have been on the estate several hundred years...".

These "several hundred years" remind us that what is happening is profoundly disturbing the ancient social and economic patterns of the countryside, which in many cases date back before the enclosure. We can sympathise with the plight of these tenants, and we can also see the monstrous amount of work such queries were generating for the Manvers Estate.

In the Manvers Collection, there are numerous letters [14] expressing contempt for Lloyd George's land reforms. R.L. Otter of Royston Manor, Retford writes August 20th 1910: "It makes me sick to think of the whole land interest in England being upset by a little creature like L. George and his followers". And again, in September 1910: "...I can't believe this infernal Lloyd George won't go down before long if the whole of the landowners in England, great and small, stand their ground absolutely firmly". Wordsworth replies: "Lloyd George's budget will have more to answer for than the country is in the least aware of as yet".

The letters make fascinating reading, reminding us of the values and alliances of an England now long gone. The Doncaster Conservative Party write to Mr Argles (Wordsworth's second in command) asking for cars to help on polling day in December 1910, as "we have a sporting chance of winning this time". From the Ditchley Estate Office in Oxfordshire, T. Wakefield writes to Wordsworth: "I feel we must all try our best to break up this gang

---

[12] The relationship between Armstrong and the Smithursts is unclear, although it is likely that Clara was William's daughter.

[13] Manvers Collection ref. MA 2C 21/115.

[14] Manvers Collection, various letters, ref. MA 2C 21.

of thieves and shall come and vote for Mr Williams. I don't yet know how to do it but I mean to come. Lord Dillon said this morning I *must* come". When the Nottinghamshire police provided a constable to stand guard at Thorsby Hall, Manver's residence, honest doubts were expressed as to the constable's suitability for Manvers' cricket team.[15] Unfortunately PC George Seston also proved somewhat officious, and did something to offend Lady Manvers. He was replaced soon afterwards but may have been relieved in more senses than one as his job standing at Manvers' gates must have been extremely boring. Finally, in an earlier (1909) letter concerning a prospective tenant for Edwinstowe House, Wordsworth [16] writes: "With regard to this house, I perhaps ought to say that a hunting man will be preferred as a tenant. Politics *must* be conservative...".

But apart from this brandishing of political ideas, much of the correspondence dealt with by The Manvers Estate at this time is to do with the complex matter of valuing and assessing the land for the new tax purposes. There is much talk of "Lloyd Georges" – the complex form provided by the Surveyor of Taxes and various land agents for different estates collaborated in devising consistent methods of responding to these.

By the summer of 1910, a slightly different class of person is moving in on the scene with the hope, no doubt, of making a killing out of the forthcoming land sales. The Manvers Estate Office is bombarded with offers from solicitors, auctioneers and valuers and surveyors, all hoping for a piece of the action.[17] Looking through the sheer quantity of such communications makes one realise just what a commercial feeding-frenzy Manvers and his trustees had set in motion.

Messrs J.H. Bradwell and Son were the auctioneers that were eventually settled on and their terms agreed, after some haggling, by R.W. Wordsworth. The dates set for the Nottinghamshire auction were 8th and 9th of March 1911 and the location, The George Hotel in Nottingham.[18]

Among the properties and land for sale was Lot 42, the farm that was to become Phoenix Farm and Lot 47, Manor Farm. As these items are of central interest to us here, I will quote from the auctioneer's catalogue [19]:

---

[15] Manvers Collection, ref. MA 2C 20/157.

[16] Manvers Collection, ref. MA 2C 163 (letter book page 544).

[17] Manvers Collection, various letters. Ref. MA 2C 21/114,119,150–3, 304, 426 etc.

[18] Nottinghamshire Archives, Document DD 296/13 and Manvers Collection MA 2D 46/2/1.

[19] Nottinghamshire Archives, Document DD 296/13 and Manvers Collection MA 2D 46/2/1.

Lot 42

An exceedingly valuable "small holding" situate in Gedling Road (Arnold Lane) in the Parish of Gedling, comprising some good feeding, Dairy and Arable land, containing an area of 68 acres, 0 roods and 11 perches or thereabouts, now and for some years past in the occupation of Mr Arthur Lamb, on a yearly tenancy determinable by 12 months' notice, expiring on any 6th April.

The Farmhouse is well placed and comfortable, occupying a good position and the accommodation comprises: Dining Room, Drawing Room, Breakfast Room, Kitchen, Scullery and 7 bedrooms.

The Brick built and tiled Farm Buildings are situate adjoining the House and include a newly constructed range of Cowhouses for 12 Cows, Barn with Granary over Loose Boxes, Cart Horse Stable, Implement Shed, Covered in Crew Yard, Stackyard etc.

This holding is practically in a ring fence and has been farmed by Mr Lamb for some years. It is in an excellent state of cultivation and forms a very compact and valuable small Dairy Holding.

Mines and minerals reserved – sold subject to the Digby Colliery Company's lease.

Lot 47

A most excellent Holding known as "Manor Farm" situate on the Gedling Road, embracing rich feeding Dairy and arable land and containing a total area of 59 acres 3 roods and 6 perches or thereabouts, now and for many years past in the occupation of Mr T.N. Parr and Mr W. Barnes; held on yearly tenancies determinable by 12 months' notice expiring on any 6th April.

The farmhouse abuts to the main Gedling Road and is a comfortable residence, built of brick and slated, and contains Dining Room, Drawing Room, kitchens, Pantry, Out offices and 6 bedrooms.

The Farm buildings consist of a Carriage House, Nag Stable, range of Cowhouses, Barn, Cart Horse Stable, Implement Shed and Sundry Boxes, together with a covered crew yard.

> This is a most desirable, conveniently situate and attractive Dairy Farm, and it has been well farmed for some years.

Jane Neave was not at the auction, but she had instructed James Holroyd, an estate agent, to bid for her. At the time she was working as Warden of University Hall in St Andrews, which is why she could not bid for herself, so she must have had a tense time waiting for the news from Nottingham. In the event, the farm was put down to her and Holroyd paid the customary 10% deposit on the £3050 she paid.

It is not surprising that the auction attracted some speculative buying, and in the case of the other lots that Jane and Ellen bought jointly, namely Manor Farm (lot 47) and lots 49, 50 and 51, small connecting parcels of land that would make the farms more practical, they were initially snapped up by other bidders. William Stickney, a Nottingham solicitor, bought Manor farm for £2070, and a local property developer, Edward Douglas, the smaller lots for £915. They both made a small but healthy profit when they sold them on to Jane and Ellen jointly in a transaction known as a sub-sale which was completed in July. Negotiations about these sales were going on between "Ellen Brookes-Smith and another" (presumably Jane) and Stickney and Douglas during May and June. Stickney saw a profit of £330 and Edward Douglas £140. The Manvers estate made £6,035 out of the whole deal, but Jane and Ellen ended up paying £6,505. This all made the conveyancing documentation a little more complex, but on July 8th 1911, Church Farm (later Phoenix Farm) and Manor Farm plus the three small plots of land became the property of Jane Neave and Ellen Brookes-Smith. Both parties owned both properties "in equal shares".[20] Although it was Jane who successfully put in the bid for Church Farm in March, when the sale is listed [21] by the Manvers Estate on 10th July, the purchasers of Church Farm (lot 42), Manor Farm (lot 47) and the additional smaller plots (lots 49, 50 and 51) are given as Ellen Brookes-Smith and Emily Jane Neave. The order of events whereby Jane and Ellen came to be joint owners of the two farms is not entirely clear, but it seems most likely that Jane was first in the field and that Ellen decided to join her in the farming enterprise shortly afterwards, perhaps in April or May.

---

[20] Manvers Collection – various letters around 2D 46 and 2C 22/92 shows details of the sales. All the conveyancing documents show "joint shares".

[21] Manvers Collection, MA 2C 22/92.

In the absence of any correspondence between the two women, it is hard to know how they managed the financial side of this arrangement. What is clear, however, is that the remaining balance after Jane's deposit of £305 for Church Farm was financed by a loan from the Capital and Counties Bank in Nottingham to the sum of £2,745.[22] So Jane had contributed roughly a half share of the whole project.

The auction had been delayed until March because of flooding that had taken place elsewhere in Nottinghamshire earlier in the year and the late date of the auction may be responsible for conflicting dates concerning Jane and Ellen's initial occupancy of the farms. On the 4th April 1911, we find a panicky letter from C.S. Preston, Jane's solicitor asking Henry Wing, Manvers' solicitor, to give notice to quit to the previous tenant. The deadline for this was 6th April (Lady Day) [23] and even if notice were given in time, Farmer Lamb would have had a year to pack up and clear out. If this deadline were missed, which it may have been, Lamb would have had two years as tenant with Jane as owner. Stickney, who had bought Manor Farm, seemed to have the matter in hand rather earlier [24] but may have neglected to act on this because he was selling the property to Ellen. In his two memoirs, Colin Brookes-Smith dates the beginning of the Phoenix Farm project as 1913 and there may be a good reason for this apparent time lapse: if Ellen missed her Lady Day deadline, she would have had to wait a further year before taking up occupancy.

In any case, Jane was still working at St Andrews University at this time, and was in no position to take up immediate residence. But because Jane is listed as "farmer" in Kelly's Directory [25] in 1912, we can safely assume that she did not have to wait another year. She would have had the farm with vacant possession on 6th April 1912. In the case of Ellen Brookes-Smith, though, her first listing as "farmer" appears in Wright's Directory in 1913 [26] so it is conceivable that some difficulty had arisen. Colin Brookes-Smith is certain that the two ladies' farming enterprise started in 1913, but this may apply just to his parents with Jane starting earlier.

---

22 Manvers Collection, MA 2D 46/4/26.

23 April 6th or Lady Day. Lady Day had originally been 1st January but in calendar changes in the 18th century, this was shifted forwards. The beginning of April for tax purposes is a remnant of this traditional date.

24 Manvers Collection, MA 2D 46/3/28/1.

25 Kelly's Directory p.77, 1912.

26 Wright's Directory p.627 1913.

The only land Manvers had sold in this area previously had been to the Great Northern Railway in 1874. The July 1911 list of buyers on a Manvers document [27] drawn up at the time of final conveyancing makes interesting reading. It shows the variety of interests that stepped in when the old aristocratic land owner sold up. As well as the private individuals like Jane Neave and Ellen Brookes-Smith, we find The Digby Colliery Company Limited, The Westdale Freehold Land Co-operative Society Ltd and the names of property developers such as Albert and Frederick Hardy. Also appearing on the list is the local industrialist John Ashworth esq.

There were winners and losers in the process of social change which is exemplified in the selling of Gedling. Some of the winners are listed above – enterprising middle class individuals with a little spare cash to speculate or invest. Also winners were the urban poor who, because of Lloyd George's People's Budget, for the first time experienced some form of social security in old age pensions, widows' pensions and unemployment pay. But what became of the tenants who could not afford to buy their properties and were given notice to leave by April 6th? Although the old aristocratic form of land ownership was essentially conservative in nature, it also, in its own way acted as an older form of social organisation. When the state old age pension came in (5 shillings per week) Manvers continued to make up his pensions to 8s 6d. The estate was also willing to intervene in questions of hardship, housing conditions and cruelty to children. When a tenant's horse became lame, efforts were made to find a replacement. Noblesse obliged in many cases where the state might take an interest today. It was a paternalistic world but privilege was matched to an extent with an awareness and acceptance of obligations. Correspondence in the Manvers Collection shows a curious balancing of the rights of the landowner and a genuine desire to do the right thing.

It would be wrong to say that the Manvers sales ended the interests of aristocratic land owners in Gedling. The church of All Hallows, for example, remained in the gift of Lord Carnarvon, and at a much later date, Lady Carnarvon donated the picturesque drinking fountain that stands just below the church where Main Road meets Arnold Lane. No doubt Gedling remained for many years an essentially conservative place where local grandees, themselves often connected to the old aristocratic families,

---

[27] Manvers Collection, ref. M3670.

arranged garden fetes and cricket matches. The Manvers Gedling sales were a symptom of social change, but by no means the final chapter in the story of the old social order.

In The Times article quoted at the beginning of this chapter, the desirability of this land for building purposes is mentioned but on the whole, we have to wait some time for this. Perhaps the advent of WW1 followed by two decades of depression and then another World War slowed the pace of development. Although there was some building on the land Hardy bought on Westdale Road (now Lane) from the 1930s onwards, the real suburbanisation of the area between Westdale Lane and Arnold Lane started slowly in the late forties and only really got going in the sixties and seventies. When Phoenix Farm was eventually demolished and built over by The Coal Board in 1953/4, the rest of the land right up to Mapperly Plains, with the exception of the golf course, was still in some form of cultivation.

Around Gedling Village, even today, it is easy to imagine a past which was, at the beginning of the 20th century, still essentially rural. The remains of farmhouses, cottages and smithies are still dotted around the area, nowadays making pleasant upmarket dwellings for the suburban inhabitants. Also in evidence are the mature fruit trees in gardens which would once have been standing in well cared for orchards. All these are evidence of a way of life that the auction of March 1911 began to finally erode.

Chapter Four

PHOENIX FARM

As the period of Jane Neave's ownership of Phoenix Farm is now firmly out of living memory, the material in this chapter is likely to give the best definitive account of the farm possible. Our sources were twofold: first, some archive research which has helped to establish dates, ownership and the path that led Jane Neave to the farm; secondly, an account of life at the farm during WW1 written by Colin Brookes-Smith, the son of Jane Neave's farming partner, Ellen Brookes-Smith, which takes the form of a nineteen page letter illustrated with forty-two annotated photographs. It is entitled *Ladies who Farmed in Gedling 1913–1923* and is in the form of an illustrated letter addressed to Mr and Mrs Dickenson who in 1982 owned Manor Farm House.

Apart from some other scanty documentary evidence, Colin's memoir is the definitive account of life at Phoenix Farm and Manor Farm during this period. He visited Gedling again in 1953 and 1979, and mentions that on his earlier visit there was "still a tradition of the ladies who farmed". In a preamble to *Ladies who Farmed in Gedling 1913–1923*, he says: "I have briefly related the history of the two farms during my parents' tenure because it fills a gap in the early part of this century which is probably little known to people living in Gedling today". Colin knew J.R.R. Tolkien, but his acquaintance with Jane Neave and Hilary Tolkien was greater. In one place in his memoir he refers to Hilary Tolkien as "the brother of the hobbit man", which suggests that Ronald was not of central interest to him. However, his daughter Jennifer prevailed on him to write down his memories of Tolkien towards the end of his life, and these memories appear in the memoir also referred to in this book entitled *Some Reminiscences of J.R.R. Tolkien*. Colin is a little vague on dates, which is understandable considering that these memoirs were produced sixty years after the event. His dates of 1913 and 1923 as the start and end of the Phoenix Farm venture are slightly questionable in the light of evidence we have found, but we have done our best to account for discrepancies; his assertion that the farms belonged to his parents is simply not correct – they were jointly owned with Jane Neave.

Jane Neave would certainly have been aware of Phoenix Farm, or Church Farm as it was then, from her earlier stay in Gedling (1905–1909).[1] In such a small community, it is probable that she knew Farmer Lamb, who was something of a fixture in the area and had kept the farm "in excellent condition". We do not know the exact circumstances by which she became aware that the farm was up for sale by auction in the spring of 1911; there were articles in The Times as well as the Nottingham Guardian about the forthcoming sales, but it may be that one of her Gedling contacts brought the sale to her attention. Jane was an eminently sociable person and it is likely that she kept up a correspondence with some former Gedling friends. She was certainly still working as the warden of University Hall in St Andrews till the summer of 1911[2] and her address on conveyancing documents is given as such. What is certain is that Jane would have brought this to the attention of Ellen Brookes-Smith, whom she had met through contact with her daughters, Doris and Phyllis, and the two women decided to embark on a joint venture.

As we have shown in the previous chapter, there was a flurry of land sales in the Gedling area in 1911, when the Manvers Estate announced a major sale of lots by auction. Archives of The Manvers Estate held by Nottingham University library for this period show preoccupation with the effects of Lloyd George's 1909 "People's Budget" and its aftermath. The combination of land tax, increased death and legacy duties and super tax hit the landed aristocracy hard. There was also a heavy tax on mineral rights, which in the case of Gedling, with its rich coal seams, were significant.

Certainly this budget from Asquith's radical Chancellor of the Exchequer served to change the pattern of land ownership in England for

1 See the chapter of Jane Neave.

2 Special Collections University of St Andrews.

good. Prior to this date, Earl Manvers' holdings in the county and elsewhere amounted to about 40,000 acres with an annual income of £50,000. By 1911, he had decided to make the best of a bad job and sell up. Although other aristocratic landowners held properties in the area, notably Lord Carnarvon, in whose gift All Hallows Church was, Manvers was the main player, and around this time he sold not only Church Farm and Manor Farm, but also areas like the Gedling cricket ground at the bottom of Shearing Hill. What happened in 1911 is an interesting indicator of the way the traditional pattern of land ownership was changing, and without this transformation from a semi-feudal to a modern society, the Phoenix Farm project would never have happened. Farmer Lamb had been a tenant of Earl Manvers, but Jane Neave and Ellen Brookes-Smith were their own masters.

Among the farms for sale were Church Farm (subsequently "Phoenix Farm") and Manor Farm, the details of which are given in the previous chapter. Both farmhouses were spacious and of unusual, even eccentric design; they were spacious buildings and included everything needed for successful mixed arable and livestock farming. Of the two buildings, Phoenix Farm was slightly larger and of higher status: farms facing the road traditionally were more important than those like Manor Farm, which is sideways on. It would not have escaped Jane's notice that the farms were potentially valuable building land, so although she paid a good price, she was unlikely to lose on her investment.

The Brookes-Smiths [3] deserve some brief mention here, as they remain a hazy entity in previous accounts of Tolkien's life. James Hector Smith had considerable inherited wealth from the sale of family land in Scotland. The name changed from Smith to Brookes-Smith when he married Ellen Brookes, the daughter of the Rector of Croft in Leicestershire and she declined to be plain "Mrs Smith". James and Ellen had land and property in the south of England, mainly Sussex, but also at least one other property at Sherwell in Devon, an eccentric house called Hornet's Castle. (Immediately after leaving Phoenix Farm, Jane took up residence there for a short time.) The Brookes-Smiths "lived in some style" according to their grand daughter and certainly did not have to work for a living; they had a car in which they took pleasure in touring; they took regular

[3] Information in this paragraph provided by Jennifer Paxman.

holidays in Switzerland and the Austrian Tyrol; their children had nannies; on Colin Brookes-Smith's birth certificate, his father's profession is given simply as "gentleman". Jane Neave came into contact with the Brookes-Smiths when she was the warden of University Hall at St Andrews, where the Brookes-Smith daughters, Phyllis and Doris, were at a nearby school run by Jane's friend Helen Preston. There was also a son, Colin, born in 1899, whose account of Phoenix Farm has been so valuable in compiling this account of the farm. Ellen's much older brother, James Brookes, a retired clergyman who had inherited the living at Croft from his father, was installed at Manor Farm and may well have lived on there after the departure of Jane and the Brookes-Smiths in 1922. Manor Farm House, which still stands on Arnold Lane, was a suitable residence for a gentleman, but having found that the fishing in the area could not compete with his accustomed game fishing in Scotland, he took to growing prize vegetables instead. Class still meant something in those days and Ellen Brookes-Smith was capable of expressing doubts about her son marrying May Woollard, whose father, when living, had been "in trade". The contact between the Brookes-Smith family and Jane Neave and the Tolkien brothers, which started in St Andrews around 1910, continued one way or another for the next fifty years.

According to Colin, the family experienced some kind of financial setback around the beginning of WW1, and their decision to try to make a go of the Gedling farms may be related to this. Neither James Hector nor Ellen were particularly experienced in agriculture, although Colin tells us that Ellen was interested in keeping poultry, which would explain the extensive area of Manor Farm set aside for poultry sheds. James was a gifted amateur engineer, but had no particular interest in farming. What is clear, is that Jane and Ellen struck up an immediate rapport, which was the basis of their joint venture at Phoenix Farm and Manor Farm.

One thing is certain: the name of the farm was changed from Church Farm to Phoenix Farm at some time between the summer of 1911 and 1912. If you look at a list of farms in trade directories for the period, they are of a strictly vernacular nature – Willow Farm, Manor Farm, Gedling Wood Farm etc. The name Phoenix with its Christian and classical associations is clearly out of kilter with the other more down-to-earth names to be found in the area. But of course, Jane Neave and the Brookes-Smiths were educated middle class types colonising an unspectacular corner of rural England. Because Jane is primarily associated with Phoenix Farm rather than Manor Farm, I am assuming that is was she who changed the name, although I have no proof of this. The name itself may have no particular significance, but I do allow myself some speculation in the next chapter.

Although there is a line drawing [4] of the rear of the farm by J.R.R. Tolkien, a photographic record of the farm exists in just a few archive photographs, including some partial views shown in Colin Brookes-Smith's illustrated letter. The whole layout is most clearly seen in a photograph [5] taken from the church spire just before the demolition of the farm. The farmhouse stands back from the road about fifty yards directly opposite Jessops Lane. On its left are the buildings for the storage of tools and machinery. Adjacent to the road in the direction of Manor Farm House, which can be seen at the bend of the road, is a square of buildings open-ended at the farm end. At the far end is the large barn, and down both sides are the cowsheds. Near to the gate is a taller building that served as a dovecote and the home for the bull. In this picture, the "crew yard" is open to the elements, although in the WW1 period, it had a corrugated iron roof. Beyond the barn and visible in some of Colin's photographs is the "stack yard" where hay was baled and threshing took place. It is really quite a spread and all this can be related to the auctioneer's advertisement mentioned earlier in the chapter.

The house itself probably dated from the middle of the 18th century, as does the neighbouring and very similar Manor Farm House (now a domestic residence). The brickwork dates it to around this time, and the blocked-off windows in both buildings, work which appears to have been undertaken around the time of building, may date it to 1741 [6], when there was a significant rise in "window tax".[7] At any rate, the Phoenix farmhouse was an impressive building, suitable for a better class of small tenant

---

[4] *J.R.R. Tolkien – Artist and Illustrator* by Wayne Hammond and Christina Scull. p.20.

[5] All Hallows Church.

[6] This date is speculative, but a record of listed building gives Manor Farm House as mid-18th century and the farmhouse at Phoenix farm is clearly roughly contemporary.

[7] Instituted by William III in 1696, this tax, also known as "glass tax" existed until 1851, when it was replaced by domestic rates. The tax led to the bricking-up of windows in the houses of those wishing to avoid it.

farmer. Around a three storey central section were built two curious five-sided wings that housed the drawing room, and dining room, both of which had octagonal bedrooms above. Above the central section were two bedrooms and a bathroom, while on the far right of the building was an extension in a less grand style which had a kitchen, a dairy on the ground floor and two additional bedrooms above. No shortage of bedrooms then, but Phoenix Farm was always a well-populated place to the extent that Manor Farm House was sometimes used as overspill. J.R.R. Tolkien and his brother Hilary shared a room with Colin Brookes-Smith there on at least one occasion. The rear of the Phoenix Farm house featured a distinctive brick pillared veranda that is partly visible on Tolkien's line drawing of the farm. Colin Brookes-Smith mentions in his 1979 illustrated letter that the drawing room and dining room had Adam fireplaces which description, as Christina Scull has kindly pointed out to me, probably uses the term "Adam" in a generic sense rather than implying the great designer made these ones.

At the front of the house was a walled and hedged lawn which ran down to the road and the back garden was variously used for flower and vegetable growing. There was also an orchard which was situated in the angle between Priory Lane and Arnold Road and is clearly visible on the 1900 map.

Tolkien's aunt Jane Neave was the mainstay of the farming operation, and Colin Brookes-Smith says that "the choice of Gedling was largely influenced by her". His *Ladies who Farmed in Gedling 1913 1923* has quite a lot to say about Jane. She is "a remarkable person" and "a brilliant academic who always wanted to try her hand at arable farming". He also says that she was the person who made the whole enterprise a success. There are a couple of photographic portraits of Jane, one showing her in working clothes, her hair wrapped in a headscarf holding her Irish terrier,[8] Mona. (Another one, taken at an earlier date shows her, again with the same dog, in her full academic robes, almost certainly taken at St Andrews.) These photographs of Jane, taken in her early forties, show her in uncompromisingly practical working clothes; her features are strong and rather masculine. In fact, she bears more than a passing facial resemblance to her famous nephew which perhaps confirms his view that he was more

[8] Jane always had a dog and various mutts are seen in photographs over the years.

of a Suffield than a Tolkien. In *Ladies who Farmed in Gedling 1913–1923* she is seen mucking in in a variety of strenuous agricultural activities. She once told Jennifer Brookes-Smith: "...that farm workers used to wear a sack over their shoulders when working in the fields, and so I had a sack, too. And that once upon a time, ladies had 'a dish of tay' in a shallow, two handled cup so I had one, too." She wasn't afraid of getting her hands dirty or sharing the experiences of her agricultural labourers.

Her farming partner, Ellen Brookes-Smith, who developed the poultry side of the farm, looks distinctly mannish with her short-cropped hair and strong masculine features. In two pictures she is seen wearing a collar, tie and jacket that might suggest she is making a statement about gender. She was "not the motherly type", Jennifer Paxman, her grand daughter suggests. The impression one gets is that the "ladies" were out to show they were the equal of men, perfectly capable of bearing the heavy burdens of agricultural work.

The wiry, bespectacled James Hector Brookes-Smith, is described thus by Colin Brookes-Smith: "My father, a competent amateur mechanic and carpenter had little interest in farming". He left that to the women. However, he was not totally redundant, and made himself responsible for maintaining the farm equipment. He also built extensive chicken pens and houses in the Manor Farm fields.

Jane, Ellen and James Hector Brookes-Smith occupied Phoenix Farm throughout the period,[9] leaving James Brookes in peace at Manor Farm except when it was needed for overspill purposes. There seems to be some fluidity over accommodation, and one incident mentioned later in this chapter finds Colin and the Tolkien brothers sharing a room at Manor Farm. Colin Brookes-Smith and Hilary Tolkien generally occupied the bedrooms over the kitchen and dairy. Several of the photographs in *Ladies who Farmed in Gedling 1913–1923* show them taking part in farming activities, although both were on active service at various times during the WW1 period. Hilary is mentioned by Colin Brookes-Smith as "an able horticulturalist who worked the large vegetable garden plot behind the house". Hilary, who had studied agriculture in 1909, visited Phoenix Farm when on leave during the WW1 period, and it is possible that Tolkien timed his visits to coincide with his brother's leave. However, Colin Brookes-

[9] According to Richard Paxman, Colin's grandson, from his grandfather's autobiography.

Smith's above comments suggest that he might have had a more permanent role to play in the post-war period.

Colin Brookes-Smith himself was fourteen years old when his parents first came to Gedling. He spent two years making 13lb shells at the Jardine munitions factory and, as he charmingly adds, "learning a lot of words that are not in the dictionary". Nottingham working class language must have been something of an eye-opener for Colin with his rather genteel background. He was called up in 1917 and spent some time in France, but his leave and later holidays, when he was a student at London University, were spent at the farm. He enjoyed the work, specialising in maintaining machinery.

Phyllis and Doris, the Brookes-Smiths' daughters, are also seen in several of the photographs in a variety of activities.

This being the time of WW1, various "land-girls" were in evidence, Margaret Goodman, Marjorie Atlee and Marjorie Allingham, who seem to have been daughters of Jane's friends. Also working on the farm was May Woollard, a local girl later married to Colin Brookes-Smith. Given Jane's pastoral experience in education, she would have been a suitable person to keep an eye on a number of young girls in an environment where romantic ideas could and often did flourish. There was also the redoubtable waggoner and ploughman Ernest Smith whose practical farming expertise earned him the generous wage for those days of £5 per week. Colin Brookes-Smith tells us that he was a Leicestershire man, and although there may be no connection, it is possible that Ellen Brookes-Smith knew of him and imported this important figure from her native county. Apart from this, casual labour was hired in on a seasonal basis, especially for hoeing and singling roots crops. Manor Farm House was occupied by James Brookes, a retired clergyman, and the very much older brother to Ellen, who devoted himself to cultivating his garden at Manor Farm House.

The non-human inhabitants of the farm were similarly diverse. The main dairy herd was of Friesian cows, but there were also a number of Jerseys, which, according to Colin Brookes-Smith were treated rather as pets. Jane had a soft spot for cows and was in the habit of giving them bizarre and stately names.[10] As well as the chickens in the Manor fields, there was a gaggle of geese and a dovecote. Pigs and sheep also feature in

[10] A photograph taken at Bag End features a cow called Valencia Ambassador.

photographs. At least three dogs are mentioned and pictured: Mona, Jane's Irish terrier, a bulldog called Mickie and Golly the Pekinese, who liked to chase sheep. Some pictures feature a joyous profusion of animal life about the farm accompanying human activity.

Work on the farm was "labour intensive with hardly any mechanisation". Three pictures show the strenuous activity of stacking the sheaves of wheat and building a haystack in the stack yard. A horse-drawn potato digger is also shown, as well as Colin Brookes-Smith himself working a hand operated potato sorter. The picture of a Sussex wagon laden with sacks of potatoes shows clearly how this was still essentially a 19th century operation. Every year, a steam-driven threshing machine was hired in and set up in the "stack yard" billowing clouds of dust. However, in 1920, the farm bought an American tractor, courtesy of a tax rebate, and Colin Brookes-Smith remarks how this revolutionised the activities of ploughing, reaping and baling. With a three-furrow self-lifting plough, according to Colin Brookes-Smith, it could do the work of ten men. Colin went on to be an engineer, and his interests in Phoenix Farm extended not only to the plough, but the gas lighting system and the thermostats in the poultry houses. He also mentions the thrilling sound of the hooter as the pit cages ascended and descended. An engineer by inclination and profession, Colin was interested in man-made aspects of the environment. When he returned to Gedling in 1979, you might have expected him to be dismayed by the housing estate on the site of the farm, but not a bit of it: he thought it very tasteful when he compared it with other mining villages and he may have had a point. "More a joy than a jolt" he says. It is worth noting that when the estate was built, it proved a draw to miners who appreciated its modern specifications and its non-regimented lay-out.

Relations with the local mining community were not always cordial. In one of his photographs, Colin Brookes-Smith notes that the stone wall of Manor Farm has been vandalised by "collier lads" and in another episode alluded to in a separate memoir[11], he gives an account of a stand-off with the local miners who were threatening to raid the orchards. J.R.R. Tolkien was a part of the defending force but chose the wrong orchard, so, in the end, it was down to the intimidating Ellen and Jane to ward off the attack. A bit of class warfare, then. Warfare of another kind also

---

[11] i.e. *Reminiscences of J.R.R.T.*

intruded into the life of the inhabitants of Phoenix Farm, not only in the presence of the land-girls, but also in efforts to help with the war effort. Colin remembers driving round the district in his father's "smaller car" in 1915 (illegally – he was under age) [12] collecting beds and furniture for a local convalescent home for wounded troops. This home was organized by Cathleen Turney, Colin informs us, "one of Sir John's daughters". One night in 1916, a Zeppelin was heard buzzing around the skies of Gedling and the Phoenix Farm people all got dressed and came downstairs to await their imminent death. They thought it was fitting to meet their fate "suitably attired", but in the end, one small bomb was dropped on neighbouring Netherfield and only a couple of windows were broken in a railway signal box.

Throughout WW1, the Phoenix and Manor Farms would have been striving for maximum productivity and may well have been highly profitable. In the last years of the war, particularly, with unrestricted naval warfare taking a heavy toll on shipping, domestic food production was essential to keep the nation from starvation. From 1916 onwards, the situation was not far from desperate, with bishops giving their flocks official dispensations for agricultural workers to work on the Sabbath. Colin Brookes-Smith's memoir only gives some slight glimpses of the farms in a war context, although that might be an interesting subject for someone to research further.

Although Colin Brookes-Smith's wonderful memoir may well have an element of nostalgia about it, it is clear that his photographs have stimulated some quite detailed memories sixty years after the Phoenix Farm and Manor Farm partnership was dissolved in 1922.[13] In addition to the picture of a hard-working farm, it is also clear that Jane and Ellen's farming project left room for some leisure activities and just plain fun at work. The two land girls are seen horse-riding on Arnold Road [14]; Hilary Tolkien throws apples into a blanket held by Jane Neave, Colin Brookes-Smith and Phyllis and Doris, a profusion of ducks, geese and hens mill around with evident interest; in another picture of a picnic taken in the

[12] Colin was born in 1899, so he wasn't terribly illegal.

[13] Colin says 1923. Electoral registers show Jane and Ellen there in the first half of 1922, but not in the second half, which suggests that this was their final year.

[14] Arnold Road, previously Gedling Road, became Arnold Lane, just as Westdale Road became Westdale Lane at a later date.

Phoenix Farm orchard, including Jane, Hilary, Brookes-Smith family, a school inspector [15] and at least one dog, Colin recalls that hens and goslings which joined the picnic got tipsy on the beer.

J.R.R. Tolkien was an occasional visitor at Phoenix Farm. We have little evidence of his presence there although he seems to have made himself useful. Colin Brookes-Smith was prevailed on to write down his memories of Tolkien in 1982, and his memories, which mainly concern the Swiss expedition of 1911, also contain a few tales about Tolkien at Phoenix Farm. These reminiscences, written down almost seventy years later are vague in their chronology, but are worth sharing for their own sake.

Colin remembers Tolkien visiting (between late 1915 and early 1916) [16] on an ancient AJS motorcycle. At this time he was a commissioned officer and had ridden over from Staffordshire where he was stationed. Colin, then sixteen or seventeen, and who was always fascinated by things mechanical, remembers the joy of being allowed to ride the motorcycle in the early morning twilight. Apart from his abortive role in repulsing the miner's "scrumping" raid in the orchard, the only other evidence we have of practical help at Phoenix Farm is the job he undertook of making a cobble-stone paving near the house.

Picnics, as we have seen, were a common form of entertainment at Phoenix Farm. Colin writes of one such: "A picnic down by the River Trent one evening ended prematurely. We had been playing a game of hide and seek with much running about and flinging ourselves flat on the ground when Ronald had the misfortune to put his face into a large cowpat. He was not amused and it took some time to get him cleaned up and less smelly".

Perhaps most telling of Tolkien's character is the final passage, which I quote here in full: "I have always been grateful to Ronald for his robust attitude to religious matters. He took them seriously but there was always an element of humour in it which he could not resist. Some years later, his description of a terrific skid on the highly polished marble floor of Farnborough Abbey during an important ceremonial procession and his difficulty not to burst out laughing is a case in point. On another occasion at Gedling, we three "boys" had been accommodated in a small room at Manor Farm as Phoenix Farm was full of visitors. I need hardly say that I am not noted for my piety but either in a sense of bravado or perhaps the

[15] Dorothy Le Couteur, who was also present on the 1911 Swiss expedition.

[16] This date range suggested by Christina Scull and Wayne Hammond.

This photograph of uncertain date shows Phoenix Farm on the left in relation to the church. The Phoenix Farm orchard can be seen on the other side of the fence.

The grave of Edwin Neave in All Hallows churchyard.

The Swiss party of 1911, suitably eccentrically dressed English people abroad. Notice pith helmets, cloaks, hobnail boots and alpenstocks. They were prepared for most things, which is a good job considering the hazards they faced. J.R.R. Tolkien in the crossed white scarf is seen in humorous mood and the tall Jane Neave with her broad-brimmed hat takes a central role.

A 1920s view of Bag End at Dormston in Worcestershire, where Jane Neave lived from 1923 to 1931. Tolkien adopted the name for the home of Bilbo Baggins in The Hobbit.

Left: A rare picture of Jane Neave, probably taken during her stay at St. Andrews, and possibly in the gardens of University Hall that she helped to improve. She is wearing her academic robes and accompanied, as she nearly always is, in posed photographs by a dog, in this case her Irish terrier Mona. Right: Jane at Bag End with her dog Dak. Uncertain date, but probably mid-1920s. Jane liked to be photographed with dogs – perhaps an innate modesty or shyness in front of the camera is at work here.

Jane Neave, in her eighties, sensibly dressed and straight as a ramrod, in the door of her caravan on Hilary Tolkien's fruit farm near Evesham.

A picnic in the orchard at Phoenix Farm. From the dress of Colin and Hilary (left) this would seem to be early days, around 1914. Jane Neave can be seen in her white blouse next to Colin with Hilary extreme left. The school inspector Dorothy Le Couteur is between Colin's two sisters. Another dog, Mickie the bulldog is featured as well as hens and chickens, which got tipsy on the beer.

John Suffield, taken at Bag End in the early 1920s when he was about ninety. This photograph again shows the brick-built east side of the building. John was a frequent visitor at Bag End throughout the 1920s.

Manor Farm House today.

A view of Phoenix Farm immediately prior to demolition in 1953/4 taken from the church tower. the crew yard has lost its roof at this time but the lay out of the farm buildings can be seen. Some rows of the new building on the Coal Board Estate can be seen in the background as can Manor Farm at the bend in the road.

Colin Brookes-Smith, 1937.

Jennifer Paxman, in the early 1950s.

The tall and rangy figure of Jane Neave is seen in the centre of this triptych showing work in the stack yard. Jane was tall and spare and immensely energetic, always mucking in with the hardest work on the farm.

Left: Jane's grave in Llanina churchyard. "In loving memory of Emily Jane Neave, died February 22nd 1963, aged 90". Right: The picturesque chapel of St. Ina in Gilfachreda, near New Quay in West Wales.

A view of the rear of Phoenix Farm taken prior to demolition.

A 1908 view from the tower of All Hallows, giving another partial view of Church Farm (later Phoenix Farm) on the left.

need for a display of religiosity in the presence of the two Roman Catholics I knelt down by my bedside ostensibly to say or pretend to say my prayers. At which point, Ronald threw a boot at my head with a roar of laughter. This, needless to say, cured me for ever of ostentatious religious practices and fitted well with my agnosticism".

In a hand written footnote to the typed memoir, Colin writes that when Tolkien told him the Farnborough story over tea at The Mitre in Oxford "he laughed so much at the recollection that he stuffed his handkerchief in his mouth (as he had, he told me, at Farnborough Abbey) and the American ladies having tea looked scandalised".

These stories are slight in content, but tell us something, perhaps, about Tolkien's boyishly playful sense of humour, always capable of self-mockery.

We can imagine the reception the young J.R.R. Tolkien would have received in this happy and industrious milieu in September 1914. It must have seemed something of an idyll, full of good companionship and down-to-earth common sense, perhaps a welcome change from the rarefied atmosphere of Oxford, or the suburbs of Birmingham. During this period before WW1, Tolkien consoled himself by escaping to a variety of pleasant locations, and Phoenix Farm had enough appeal to find him visiting three times at least. Again and again in his published letters, Tolkien makes it clear that his heart lies in the English West Midlands countryside. His real heartland was Worcestershire, ancestral home of the Suffields, but the ancient, homely, unpretentious village of Gedling, which was pretty without being spectacular, was also his kind of place. It is perhaps not too fanciful to imagine him sitting down to dinner in that rather grand dining room in a friendly and extended company and later retiring to his room and getting to work on the poem that was to unlock his great future work. Looking up Arnold Road to the west in the evening or over the church spire in the morning, he may even have seen the bright planet Venus low in the sky. In the third week of September 1914 there was an autumnal nip in the air, but the skies had been gloriously clear since August.[17]

---

[17] My meteorological evidence from Siegfried Sassoon's *Memoirs of a Fox Hunting Man*. Admittedly Sassoon is referring to Kent, but this kind of high pressure system is likely to have been dominant further north as well. The poets Robert Frost and Edward Thomas holidayed in similar weather in Gloucestershire/Herefordshire in the late summer of 1914.

Chapter Five

THE GEDLING POEM[1]

In a letter[2] of 1916, Tolkien describes how a meeting with his old school friends in December 1914 had helped to trigger a surge in creativity that lasted the whole period of WW1 and beyond. At the time, he was in the process of producing a further draft of *The Voyage of Eärendel the Evening Star*[3], the poem he wrote in Gedling. (It is the final draft[4] that is discussed here. Minor changes were made to the original Gedling draft, but nothing that changes its main drift.)

The words he uses to describe his feelings are interesting – "pent up things" and "a tremendous opening up of everything for me" – which betray strong psychological forces at play. It would not be unusual for a twenty two year-old undergraduate who was, at the time, undergoing a series of personal crises, to find an outlet for his emotions in poetry; what is extraordinary about the poem he wrote in Gedling, is the way it introduces for the first time a character who was "first of heroes"[5] in Germanic mythology and also the first in Tolkien's great body of legends.

In this chapter, I want to explore the poem, with particular emphasis on those ideas that Tolkien carried forward into his later writings, particularly *The Lord of the Rings* and *The Silmarillion*.

There are undoubtedly some strong contextual factors that contribute to the writing of the poem, some of which are fairly clear, but some of which

---

1 For copyright reasons, it is not possible to print or quote at length from the poem The Voyage of Eärendel the Evening Star. The best source of information on the genesis of the poem and the poem itself are in *The Book of Lost Tales Part Two*.

2 *Letters*, p.10.

3 For variant spellings and their significance see my endnote 112.

4 Probably produced in 1924.

5 Grimm – *Teutonic Mythology Volume 1* p.374 referring to the Heldenbuch.

must remain in the domain of reasonable speculation. In many ways, Tolkien's life at this time was unsettled. One decision he had already made concerned his military service; at a time when his old school friends were enlisting in the armed forces, Tolkien made it clear in a letter of August that year that he had made up his mind to continue with and finish his degree, although he was probably still mulling over the matter during his stay at Phoenix Farm. Whenever his decision was finally made, it was undoubtedly one that would have caused him some heart-searching in an atmosphere which pressurised young men to embrace their patriotic duty. It was, he says in a letter of 1941, "a nasty cleft to be in".

During the Indian summer of 1914, when the glorious weather lasted well into October, it was still possible to take a romantic view of the war. In September, when Tolkien visited Phoenix Farm, the stalemate of the Western Front was just coming into being, and although newspaper reports bore news of losses on the Marne, these losses were relatively modest and there was still an atmosphere of jingoistic optimism. This deep current of patriotic feeling was all-pervasive and hard to resist. It certainly carried along Hilary Tolkien and Tolkien's school friends, and can be witnessed in the writings of Rupert Brooke and the more sober-sided Siegfried Sassoon. No one realised how awful the next four years would turn out to be.

It is possible to speculate that the element of heroism [6] that is dominant in *The Voyage of Eärendel the Evening Star* compensates for the author's own perception of his lack of heroism. Tolkien was by nature cautious and pragmatic, with little taste for war or military things; he wrote again and again about his loathing for war in his letters, not only the waste and horror of it, but his own unsuitability as a warrior. Among other things, he was temperamentally resistant to any form of military discipline – "bossing about" as he put it. In the first months of WW1, however, he would have found little sympathy for these views; it is likely that there was family pressure to enlist and Jane Neave probably shared this view. Typically, the relatives of young men at this time were simply anxious to see them "doing the right thing". In a letter of 1941 [7] to Michael Tolkien, he speaks of "hints becoming outspoken from relatives". To his friends Tolkien had pleaded

[6] John Garth's *J.R.R. Tolkien and the Great War* gives a very full account of the question of heroism in Tolkien's poetry at this time.

[7] *Letters*, p.53

poverty, pointing out that his future career depended on his getting a first class degree, and his old school friend Rob Gilson, at least, swallowed the idea,[8] taking the charitable view. When he returned to Oxford, he found a compromise solution which involved his undertaking training while studying, but his subsequent military career, which consisted of a long period of recovery from trench fever, following a brief period on the Somme, meant that he only saw limited service in various dreary camps on the East Coast. This debilitating illness was genuine but his wife and his friend Christopher Wiseman encouraged him to do everything he could to stay away from The Front and it seems that his instinct for life was the force that ultimately took control in his war years. This instinct was fortunate as the rest of his fighting unit disappeared off the face of the earth in 1918 during the Germans' last push.

At least we can surmise that for Tolkien the whole question of military service was a fraught one and one that would have been at the forefront of his mind in September 1914. It is true, though, that without the academic career he was aiming at, the prospect of earning a living and supporting a wife would have been more problematic. The long and tortured saga of his relationship with his fiancée was on hold at the time: earlier in the year, she had made the necessary conversion to Catholicism, but the affair was in limbo, with Edith living in Warwick and Tolkien shuttling between Oxford, Birmingham and a number of temporary locations with friends and relatives. It must have been a cause of frustration but repressed sexual feelings can be a good creative motivator.

One of these temporary locations was Phoenix Farm, which he had already visited at least once in 1913. Here he would have found reassuring things – a pleasant semi-rural location, a houseful of convivial friends and relatives, all presided over by his favourite aunt, Jane Neave. Jane was forty two years old at the time; she had fifteen years of teaching experience behind her in addition to her recent pastoral work at The University of St Andrews; she had her own personal experience of a difficult love-life. In short, she was the kind of person in whom her young nephew might confide, or, looking at it another way, the kind of person

---

[8] A letter from Rob Gilson quoted by John Garth in *Tolkien and the Great War*, p.44 Tolkien liked to make much of his poverty at this time and in later references to his early years, and although it is true that life at Oxford University put some strains on his purse, his poverty was always relative rather than absolute.

who might make free with her wisdom. Jane may have been stern or consoling, but it is reasonable to speculate that she may have had something to say on the subjects that preoccupied the young author, possibly the situation with Edith and the question of his military service, and possibly his poetry too, for the St Andrews documents suggest that Jane was widely read and knowledgeable in that field. Tolkien may have noted with interest that the name Jane had chosen for Phoenix Farm was also the title of another poem in *The Exeter Book*, which also contains *Crist*. It is a poem of singular beauty which draws a parallel between the mythical Phoenix and the risen Christ. Unusually for an Old English poem, it lingers in an almost romantic way over a paradisal landscape. Given Jane's deep involvement with Christian ideas and her wide knowledge of poetry, this choice of name *may* have had some deeper significance, although it is also possible that it simply signified a new and hopeful venture. The possibility remains, however, that Jane may have known about the poem through her contact with her nephew. In a very much later letter of 18th July 1962,[9] Tolkien regales Jane with a quite detailed account of his attempt to render the elaborate verse form of the medieval elegy *Pearl* into modern English. When he says "As these things interest you",[10] he may be referring to devotional poetry or just poetry, but either way the letter suggests that Jane had an abiding interest in one or both of these subjects.

It is possible to trace Tolkien's artistic and literary development since 1911, the year he went up to Oxford, in some detail. Wayne Hammond and Christina Scull's excellent *J.R.R. Tolkien – Artist and Illustrator* presents us with examples of Tolkien's weird and sometimes disturbing pictures from this period. He is preoccupied with landscapes which are both awesome and disturbing, one of which, entitled *The End of the World*, has a tiny matchstick man apparently stepping off the white cliffs of Dover into a lurid sunset. There is a strong expressionist element in these pictures, which suggests a soul in a state of flux and uncertainty, undoubtedly a by-product of post-adolescent angst. *Eeriness and Beyond* [11] is another title that suggests a self-indulgent sense of alienation. Tolkien spent, or perhaps wasted, endless hours doodling in a variety of media in his early months at Oxford, profoundly

---

9 *Letters*, p.315.

10 *Letters*, p.317.

11 *J.R.R. Tolkien Artist and Illustrator* pp.42–43.

unhappy with his original subject choice of classics. However, by September 1914, he had completed four terms in the Oxford School of English and had become deeply immersed in his study of Old and Medieval English, a subject which suited him much better and was to become his life's work.

Another factor that undoubtedly contributes to the imagery of his Gedling poem is the recent holiday he had spent in the company of Father Vincent Reade, a friend and Catholic priest, on the Lizard Peninsula in Cornwall. Barely a month previously, Tolkien had been impressed by the elemental western landscape of Cornwall, and this imagery not only pervades *The Voyage of Eärendel the Evening Star* but becomes an important element in his later mythology. The west takes on enormous significance in his mature mythology as the location of Valinor, the home of the Valar. Here Tolkien follows a well established European tradition of seeking a transcendent world beyond the ragged margins of the western coastline, whether it be Lyonesse, Avalon, the classical Hesperides, or indeed even the Atlantis myth, with which Tolkien had something of a preoccupation.

His poetry was, and remained, throughout his life, decidedly conservative in form, borrowing heavily from the verse-forms of Romantic and Victorian poetry. It would be wrong to criticise Tolkien for not being a modernist – something he never intended to be – but his early poems were often laden with artificial imagery and diction, ineptly trotting out rhythms more suitable to musical-hall [12] recitation than to his dreamily romantic themes. His friends told him to tone it down and they were right, but Tolkien at this time was a novice and as his writing career progressed, his poetry settled down into an engaging and entertaining mode perfectly integrated with his enormous talent for story-telling. In context, it can be very powerful, adding emotional resonance to his tales. Nevertheless, in these fledgling years, much of this early poetry displays a desperate exhibitionism. *The Voyage of Eärendel the Evening Star* did not on its own signal the end of this kind of vapid aesthetic, but in it Tolkien discovered a new more virile note, combining verse form and content in a workable fashion and, in its reference to the joys and sorrows of humanity, beginning to touch on mysterious deeper themes which go beyond the merely picturesque.

---

[12] As well as his fondness of Edwin Neave's music-hall banjo playing, Maggie Burns has discovered that King Edward's School drama productions were also flavoured with "music hall tunes". Without wishing to suggest this as the actual source, the rhythm of the poem *Goblin Feet* bears an unnerving resemblance to Gus Ellen's music hall classic *If It Wasn't for the 'Ouses in Between*.

His starting point for *The Voyage of Eärendel the Evening Star* was his discovery of the lines quoted below, hidden away in *Crist,*[13] a lengthy devotional poem by the eighth-century Anglo-Saxon poet Cynewulf'.[14] It was, perhaps, not an original discovery, as those particular lines merit extensive footnotes in several existing editions of the poem, and are quoted in full in Grimm's Teutonic Mythology,[15] a work with which Tolkien was surely acquainted. As with Tolkien, the interest for these previous editors and commentators had been the word/name Éarendel, which does not have any clear derivation in Old English, and the Bosworth and Toller dictionary only cites the one instance of its use in *Crist.*

Éala, Éarendel, engla boerhtast, *(Hail Eärendel, brightest of angels)*
Ofer middangeard monnum sended *(Sent to men over middle-earth)*
And sôðfæsta sunnan leoma *(true ray of the sun)*
Torht ofer tunglas, thu tîda gewhane *(radiant over the stars, who for all time)*
Of sylfum the symle inlîhtes *(shine ever by your own light)*

Tolkien was attracted to and intrigued by the name Éarendel and I have much more to say on the provenance of this word/name in the chapter entitled *The Name Eärendel.* For the time being, suffice it to say that the search for the meaning of this mysterious name was exactly the kind of puzzle that would have appealed to Tolkien. He had excelled at Oxford in his philological studies and we can see how this process of digging in the linguistic past for meanings and stories suited his temperament. The reward for this kind of painstaking study is imaginative access to an altogether different world of heroes and adventure and Tolkien came to be defined by these two poles of the personality – the homely, almost absurdly suburban professor on the one hand, and the extraordinary writer of imaginative fiction on the other. But the link between his profession and his imaginative life was an entirely natural one and in a letter of 1956,[16] he suggests that it was in 1914 that this meeting of academic and creative worlds began.

[13] Crist is in three parts, known as I, II and III. The passage in question occurs in the second section of the second part of "Crist I". For convenience here, I just refer to it as "Crist".

[14] The authorship is uncertain but may be that of the one named Anglo-Saxon poet, Cynewulf.

[15] *Grimm Volume 1,* p.375.

[16] *Letters,* p.231.

Those few lines from an obscure eighth century devotional poem were the lines that unlocked Tolkien's imagination and led directly to the writing of *The Voyage of Eärendel the Evening Star*. Out of context, they suggest immediately why Tolkien might have felt attracted by them – the heroic greeting, the mission of the angel and the term "middle-earth", a commonplace term in Old English, which has now become firmly associated with Tolkien's mythology.

In the poem written at Phoenix Farm, Eärendel is a personification of the evening star in his journey from sunset, through the night, eventually to be extinguished in the light of the sun. He is imagined as a bold and heroic mariner sailing through the heavens and meeting a tragic end. In a story that tests our powers of visualisation, Tolkien tries to suggest the actual course of the Evening Star through the sky, as it would occur in a flat-earth cosmos, lingering in the twilight and then dipping below the horizon to travel eastwards, past the moon and constellations, towards the rising sun where his light is extinguished. The imagery, which combines celestial and maritime elements – the constellations become "argosies" – suggests a throwback to a pre-scientific Germanic world in which the greatest adventures were by sea.

Tolkien employs a tight eight-line verse form throughout. It is an elaborate piece of versification, employing alternate lines with internal rhyming ("arose" and "flows") with rhyming alliterative lines such "Where the **sh**ores are **sh**eer and dim".

The rhythm has a driving quality, based on the traditional English common metre (alternate four stress and three stress lines), but adding extra short syllables in a regular pattern that give it extra pace and airiness.[17] There is a sense of urgency and direction about the way Tolkien is writing which anticipates a more mature style.

The element of alliteration was a common feature of all Old English poetry, and the internal rhyming in this context may owe something to Layamon's *Brut*, a Middle English poem Tolkien would have known, the content of which deals with a similar reckless heroism. On the other hand, this technique has always been a favourite of those trying their hand at

---

[17] Technically a mixture of iambic and anapaestic feet with lines tending to start with the lighter anapaest (two unstressed followed by one stressed syllable). These Greek terms do not square easily with English poetry, but the effect of the pairs of unstressed syllables is to add pace and urgency to the poem.

mocking up an old ballad, everyone from Coleridge in *The Rime of the Ancient Mariner* to Lewis Carroll in *Jabberwocky*. Apart from these features, the tightly organised syllabic form owes more to Victorian versification, the kind of thing that would have come relatively easily to the turn-of-the-century schoolboy thoroughly versed in the metrical niceties of classical poetry. But the virtue of *The Voyage of Eärendel the Evening Star* is the way in which Tolkien successfully combines these two elements – the direct and visceral quality typical of Germanic myth with the more fanciful and picturesque Victorian elements. You could say that the whole of Tolkien's writing depends on a combination of these two elements in one form or another. Mythical material can be rather colourless, overburdened with names and incident, and *The Silmarillion* could be accused of this failing. However, *The Lord of the Rings* may well have earned its popularity with a wider public partly because of its intensely realised landscapes and other visual detail.

Tolkien was always modest about his poetic ability, perhaps sensing that some would say that some of the early poems especially erred in matters of taste. Typically it continued to be conservative in nature, consciously embracing the traditional features of rhythm and rhyme. Tolkien enthusiasts may be well disposed towards it all but the neutral observer will find much to criticise. He was gracious enough to acknowledge his readers' enthusiasm and the enjoyment he obviously took in writing his verse is its own best recommendation. Later in life he rejected some of his apprentice poems such as *Goblin Feet* [18] but was scrupulous in his revisions of the poems he decided to publish. But whatever we think of Tolkien's poetry as such, the content of the poem we are considering will immediately ring a few bells with those acquainted with Tolkien's subsequent mythology.

For a start, there is the heroic and reckless Eärendel, who is to become an important figure in later writing. This four-syllable name [19] is typical of many he invented in his Elvish language, Quenya. In a much later lecture entitled *Welsh and English*,[20] Tolkien tellingly refers to the sound of "cellar door",[21] which, regardless of its meaning, is a beautiful sounding phrase, the kind of

---

[18] In 1971, "I wish the unhappy little thing, representing all I came (so soon after) to fervently dislike, could be buried forever". Quoted from *www.tolkienlibrary.com/press/oxfordpoetry1915.htm*

[19] Tolkien indicates that the first two letters are separate although elided phonemes through his use of the dieresis on the "a". In other Old English texts, the acute accent over the "E" indicates that the first two letters are not a diphthong. A secondary stress goes on the third syllable.

[20] *The Monster and the Critics*, p.191.

[21] Curiously the "cellar door" idea reappears in Richard Kelly's 2001 film *Donnie Darko*.

which are more common in Welsh than English. So for Tolkien the discovery of the aesthetically pleasing Old English word/name Éarendel [22] was notable.

There is also an evocation of majestic landscapes on a cosmic scale – "the shores are sheer and dim", "the mouth of night", "the last and lonely sand". These melancholy images of evening and darkness, often associated with the West, here "Westerland", are evoked throughout the *Silmarillion* and *The Lord of the Rings*. Here we see the evidence of his recent Cornish holiday. What might be seen as a fairly conventional dalliance with a nostalgic and picturesque "Celtic twilight" may start here, but in its final form, it imbues *The Lord of the Rings* with a truly powerful spiritual quality.

As he appears in later writing, Eärendil here is a wanderer, a "wayward spirit" on a heroic mission and involved in "lonely errantry". His association with the Evening Star here also prefigures the Silmaril that he will eventually carry on his forehead before he is granted a kind of immortality by the gods of Valinor. In the third verse, he is described as faring over the "jewelled" waste and Eärendel or, as he is subsequently spelled Eärendil, is commonly associated with the jewels of the stars.[23] In *The Voyage of Eärendel the Evening Star*, this mythical content is suggested by such phrases as "a ray of light", "a silver spark", "a silver flame" and "an isled lamp". He even has his ship (eventually called Vingelot or Wingelot in the Silmarillion), his "gleaming galleon", and his "argent-timbered bark". In later versions of the story, Eärendel's boat is specifically built from a pale coloured wood. At this early stage, however, there is some vagueness about the nature of the boat – is it really a galleon, and if so, why does it also have oars? A Viking ship would have had both sail and oars, and perhaps this was the image he had in mind in 1914, but this was twenty five years before the stunning Anglo Saxon Sutton Hoo ship was discovered.

In the Sun and the Moon, we are reminded of the creation of these objects in *The Silmarillion* to give light to Elves and Men, after the two light-giving trees of Valinor have been poisoned and their light imprisoned in the Silmaril. Representations of the sun and moon have a mysterious symbolic resonance in Tolkien's contemporary drawings and paintings,

---

[22] *Letters*, p.385.

[23] *The Silmarillion*, p.301. "...and Eärendil the Mariner sat at the helm, glistening with the dust of elven- gems"; also similar references in *The Book of Lost Tales* to Eärendel arising from the "diamond dust" of Kor.

sometimes appearing in ludicrous proximity. But these landscapes, as part of the cosmos Tolkien is formulating, are not bound by logical rules.

Apart from the 1914 *Voyage*, there are several other versions of the story of Eärendel that the reader might encounter in Tolkien's work. Early in 1915, he starts to write *The Shores of Faery*,[24] in which we can already see many of the names and mythical elements that occur in the mature mythology – Valinor, Taniquetil and Eglamar as well as Eärendel's ship, now named Wingelot. The "two trees" of Valinor, whose essence is captured in the Silmaril also make their first appearance. The verse is less exuberant than that of *The Voyage of Eärendel the Evening Star*, and clearly owes more to his evolving Quenya language and a developing mythical narrative. Its style shows echoes of Keats and Tennyson, but like *The Voyage of Eärendel the Evening Star*, it is fully coherent and, if anything, more restrained as it beds down into a larger narrative.

In a passage in *The Fellowship of the Ring*, in the chapter entitled *Many Meetings*, Frodo dreams a much-elaborated version of the story sung by the disembodied voice of Bilbo. This version crams in a whole episode of Tolkien's developed mythology. Like much of the poetry in *The Lord of the Rings*, it hints at a mythical past quite beyond the ken of the average hobbit. But the source of this poem is the story of Eärendil, initially developed in 1916, that eventually finds its way into *The Silmarillion*. This prose version contains a fully developed version of the original. The chronology of Tolkien's work is famously tricky, as the material in "The Silmarillion"[25] was developed over a period of fifty years with lots of tinkering on the writer's part. What we can see here, however, is the full development of a vague idea into a fully rounded piece of mythology.

In Chapter 24 of *The Silmarillion*, *Of the Voyage of Eärendil and the War of Wrath*, we find the fully developed story of the star-sailor that started at Phoenix Farm. Eärendil sails into the west to enlist the help of the Valar against the powers of Morgoth. He succeeds in his quest, but having entered forbidden territory he cannot be allowed to return to middle earth. In recognition of his brave mission, he is rewarded with a kind of immortality "most often seen at morning or at evening" in his ship Vingelot, which "passed through the Door of Night even into the oceans of

[24] *The Book of Lost Tales Part Two*, p.271.

[25] "The Silmarillion" in quotation marks denotes the whole rambling body of work that eventually found its way into *The Silmarillion*, in italics, published in 1977.

heaven". (Notice "the mouth of night" in the original poem.) The last chronological reference to Eärendil in *The Lord of the Rings* comes in Galadriel's gift to Frodo, a phial of water containing light from the star of Eärendil, which he uses to give light in the lair of Shelob the spider. Frodo's Elvish invocation of the power of the light of Eärendil has strong echoes of the lines in *Crist*. Slightly earlier than this, in the chapter entitled *The stairs of Cirith Ungol*, Sam Gamgee comes to the realization that the gift of Galadriel literally contains the light of Eärendil from the old tale. "Why to think of it," he says, "we're in the same tale still!" So the idea of Eärendil spans the whole of Tolkien's writing career but all those elements were there, partly realised, in the poem of 1914.

There are numerous other references to Eärendel or Eärendil in the works of J.R.R. Tolkien, too numerous to mention within the scope of this short book. Suffice it to say, Eärendel or Orentil was, according to Jacob Grimm, the "first of heroes" in Germanic mythology and also fulfilled a similar role in Tolkien's mythology. (Tolkien himself describes it as the start of his mythology, although in the same passage, he describes the story of Beren and Luthien as the *kernel* of it).[26]

What Tolkien did during the years of WW1 and beyond, was to explore the ramifications of his poem by inventing a cycle of stories in which Eärendel has an important role. Material that bubbled up semi-consciously in Gedling underwent a process of rationalization over years of writing and rewriting until it attained a coherent form in his mythology. Some of the ideas that entered his later body of legends were probably simmering in his mind before he wrote *The Voyage of Eärendel the Evening Star*, but it is fair to consider the poem of September 1914 as the first bold brushstroke in a picture that only later took form. As Wayne Hammond and Christina Scull point out in *The J.R.R. Tolkien Companion and Guide*,[27] it is unlikely that Tolkien saw his poem at the time as fitting into a larger body of legend, and in one version, the name Phosphorus (light-bearer) is substituted for Eärendel. It is indisputable, however, that within a couple of years, the figure of Eärendel had assumed massive importance.

In a much later letter, Tolkien describes how the story that was eventually to become *The Lord of the Rings* started not in 1937, when he wrote the first sentence of that great work, but in 1914, with the writing of

---

[26] *Letters*, p.221.

[27] *The J.R.R. Tolkien Companion and Guide* p.234.

The Voyage of Eärendel the Evening Star. The poem and the later story, he says, were both part of the same process that the war "spurred into growth".

The Voyage of Eärendel the Evening Star represents a significant leap forward in Tolkien's literary development, both in form and content. The great upheaval of the world war may have provided the troubled psychic energy that fuels the poem, but Phoenix Farm certainly had a role to play as well. What we now know about the ambience of the farm, presided over by his wise and cultured aunt Jane Neave, made it a perfect place for the germination of a mythology. It was a temporary haven in Tolkien's troubled life.

Chapter Six

THE NAME EÄRENDEL[1]

One has to be cautious when considering the origin of Tolkien's mythological names, if for no other reason than the author himself dismissed such attempts as merely "private amusements"[2] which were "valueless for the interpretation or elucidation of my fiction". In *The Book of Lost Tales Part Two*, after a discussion of the origins of the name Eärendel, Christopher Tolkien points us to a passage in *The Fall of Gondolin* which teasingly says that there are many interpretations of the name, but that ultimately its meaning remains a mystery.[3]

It is true that Tolkien scholarship is littered with fanciful interpretations from writers whose search for cryptic meanings borders on the lunatic. On the other hand, an examination of the name Eärendel does tell us something about the very earliest days of Tolkien's myth-making career. This concerns the way his writing is founded in language (or languages) and the way he accumulates a cluster of meanings around a linguistic investigation, in this case, into the meaning of the word Eärendel.

My own investigation into the route Tolkien may have taken is based on the assumption that when starting out on his philological career, as he had the year before he wrote *The Voyage of Eärendel the Evening Star*, he would have taken the line of least resistance and looked for the kind of ready-made material it was possible for me, as an amateur in this field, to find in a few days in a university library. I may be wrong, but I believe this account,

---

1 Variant spellings: in Old English texts the name is rendered "Éarendel" but Tolkien chooses to use the dieresis in "Eärendel" in his early spellings of the name to indicate the same thing – the separate but elided initial vowels. When the name becomes part of his Elvish language, it became" Eärendil". I have tried to be consistent with the different contexts of the word.

2 *Letters*, p.380.

3 *The Book of Lost Tales*, p.267.

which is simpler than those of other dedicated Tolkien scholars,[4] may be truer to process than Tolkien hints at in his letters.

Perhaps it is true that to enjoy the fiction one does not have to know the origin of the name, but in the case of Eärendel there is a clear and interesting story, partly recounted by Tolkien himself in a letter of 1967. Tolkien describes how he came across the name in the poem *Crist* by the eighth century English poet Cynewulf. Cynewulf is interesting to Old English scholars for several reasons, not the least of which is that he is the only named poet of the period. He is a self-confessed [5] misery, writing, as he tells us, at night, by the light of a single candle, pouring out pious lamentations about sin and judgment at the end of the world. (The name Cynewulf is cryptically encoded in runes in his poetry, a touch Tolkien would have liked.) As for *Crist*, Tolkien dismissed the poem as a whole as "a lamentable bore" but singled out, or so he tells us, a few lines that caught his attention. The first two lines read as follows:

> Éala Éarendel, engla beorhtast (Hail Eärendel, brightest of angels)
> ofer middangeard monnum sended (sent to men over middle-earth)

Tolkien says that he was struck by the beauty of the "word (or name)" éarendel, for at that point, he was not clear which it was. Compared with most Anglo Saxon words, it was "euphonic to a peculiar degree".[6] This is, indeed the case: most Old English names are mono- or duo-syllabic and this polysyllabic name is more in keeping with the Celtic or Finnish names that Tolkien felt had more of an aesthetic appeal. In his later writing, when he had "adopted the word into my mythology" by giving it an Elvish meaning (ear-endil = sea lover) we notice this syllabic pattern occurring again and again in his invented names.

If he was, as John Garth [7] suggests, consulting the third volume of Grein and Wulcker's *Bibliotek der Angelsachsischen Poesie* in September 1914, he would have found no explanatory footnotes on the name, so at this point,

---

[4] Notably Carl Hostetter's *Over Middle-earth Sent Unto Men* (Spring 1991 Mythlore). This learned article goes way beyond my purposes in this book, but will be interesting for those looking for a more detailed account of the philology in question.

[5] See the autobiographical coda to his poem *Elene* in the *Vercelli Book*. Project Gutenberg provide a downloadable translation by Lucius Holt (1881).

[6] *Letters*, p.385.

[7] *Tolkien and the Great War*, p.44.

he might have referred to the standard Bosworth and Toller Old English dictionary, where he would have found the definition "A shining light, ray". There is nothing in the make-up of the word to suggest a clear derivation and Tolkien followed the reasonable theory that this was a personal name. Pursuing this line of thought, he referred to *The Blickling Homilies*, a series of Old English sermons that had been published in 1883. Here he found another rare occurrence of the name in Old English which uses the formula "se niwa eorendel" (the new eorendel) to refer to John the Baptist. This was an association which resonated throughout *The Voyage of Eärendel the Evening Star*: just as John the Baptist is the harbinger of Christ, so the evening/morning star (Venus) is the harbinger of dawn. The use of the word "new" here is intriguing: on the one hand, "eorendel" may denote a common noun denoting "the (new) dawn"; on the other hand, it may suggest that the "eorendel" is being used as a personal name of a hero referring back to memories of a dim Teutonic past. The extent to which the readers of (or listeners to) *The Blickling Homilies* would have recognised the word as a proper noun is unclear, in the same way, for instance, that the modern reader might take the word "pandemonium" as a common noun denoting a state of uproar or as a specific place in Milton denoting the home of the fallen angels. It is possible that the Anglo Saxon audience may have recognised the name of a hero: typical of Old English poetry is its tendency to assign heroic qualities to Christian figures, as in *The Dream of the Rood*, for example, where Christ is seen heroically leaping onto the cross to embrace his divinely ordained fate. Although Tolkien specifically rejects the idea that Eärendel has any Christian associations in his poem, this association with John the messenger, like the angel in *Crist*, carried a general symbolic significance. In his daringly titled book *Tolkien Author of the Century*, Tom Shippey [8] points out the similarity between the passage in Cynewulf and a Latin antiphon which begins "O Oriens". The passage in *Crist* is not a close translation of the antiphon in question,[9] although the material is related and "Oriens", denoting the morning star, may have suggested an additional phonological link with Eärendel.

It may be that when he came to write the Gedling poem, Tolkien had enough to go on with the "ray of light" dictionary definition and the

[8] *J.R.R. Tolkien Author of the Century*, p.257.

[9] "O Morning Star, splendour of light eternal and sun of righteousness: Come and enlighten those who dwell in darkness and the shadow of death".

association with John the Baptist as the harbinger of the Son of God. However, in the letter of 1967 where he discusses the name "Eärendel" and its importance in his work, he describes how he took his investigation further.

As I have suggested, the Grein and Wulcker compendium of Anglo Saxon poetry has nothing to say on the subject. However, just about every other editor of Cynewulf's *Crist* does include some useful footnotes. It would be surprising if Tolkien had not consulted the original classic edition of the poem by the great Anglo Saxon scholar and philologist Benjamin Thorpe; in his 1842 edition, Thorpe says: "The word Éarendel occurs with the signification of jubar (Venus) in the glossary of Moyen Moutier". It is unlikely that Tolkien would have referred to this 18th century demonology, but at least he had a clear association with a heavenly body, and specifically the evening star, Venus.

The footnote in Israel Gollancz's 1892 edition of *Crist* is far more helpful and it is worth quoting it in full:

> "...Éarendel, it is difficult to translate the word adequately; some bright star is evidently meant, probably the same as *Orvandels-ta*, "Orwendel's toe," mentioned in the Edda. Thor carried Orwendel from Jotunheim in a basket on his back; Orwendel's toe stuck out of the basket and got frozen; Thor broke it off, and flung it at the sky, and made a star of it, which is called Orvandels-ta; (Grimm's Deutsche Myth.) That the story of Orwendel was Christianised in medieval times is attested by the German story of Orendel in the Heldenbuch, where the hero wins "the seamless coat" of his master. Eärendel does not occur elsewhere in A.S. poetry as a poetical designation of Christ; the word is interpreted in the Epinal glossary by "jubar". The spelling in the Efurt Gloss "oerendil" is noteworthy. It seems probable that "Eärendel" = Orion, the constellation brightest in winter-time, and "Orvandels-ta" = Rigel, the chief star of the constellation".

Gollancz also rightly points out that there is a reference throughout to the opening of John's Gospel. Here is virtually everything Tolkien wanted to know and the similarity between the Gollancz footnote and the content of the 1967 letter suggests to me that this might well have been one of his sources.

If Tolkien did not consult Gollancz, he may well have gone to the acknowledged source of his footnote, Jacob Grimm's *Teutonic Mythology*. Given his burning interest in Germanic mythology, it is unlikely that he did not consult Grimm at some point.

In the chapter on heroes towards the end of the first volume, Grimm devotes three pages to Orentil (the spelling of the name, as you will have noticed, is subject to great variation). Included in this engaging stroll around the legends is everything in Gollancz, but also reference to Éarendel as a kind of Germanic proto-Ulysses, a much travelled mariner. He is the first of the Germanic heroes, and the stories may find their origin in a very dim Germanic prehistory. Interestingly, Grimm quotes the exact lines from *Crist* that interested Tolkien so much. Grimm, as usual, indulges in some tenuous etymology, but concludes, as most commentators do, that the origin of the name is obscure. Significantly, though, he misses the possible presence of the Old English root "ear = sea", a connection that Tolkien did make at some point, incorporating "ear" with the same meaning into his Elvish glossary. It is, however, rather curious that Tolkien does not mention these identical Old English and Elvish forms at any point.

Having ascertained all this, Tolkien now has a heady mix of associations, all of which, in one way or another go to establish the identity of the Old English Éarendel and his own heroic figure Eärendil (ear = sea, endil = lover of). Those associations are: the hero messenger; the bearer of light; the mariner; the star, either Rigel or the planet Venus. Tolkien's eventual interpretation of the name derives from a cluster of possible meanings rather than one fixed interpretation. At the end of the 1967 "drafts for a letter to Mr Rang" Tolkien clearly states [10] that it is only in his name Eärendil that the actual source of the name has any significance. So it seems that for this very first step in his mythological journey, Tolkien needed to gather together these associations as the foundation of his poem. He borrows names elsewhere from old Germanic literature, notably the name Gandalf and those of his dwarves from the Icelandic Edda, but nowhere else does he borrow the whole character.

Although it would be churlish to doubt the broad outline of Tolkien's account of his discovery of the identity of Eärendel, it is possible that his claim to have singled out these few lines in Cynewulf's *Crist* is a little

[10] *Letters*, p.387.

ingenuous. Anyone who has read the poem will find the lines no more or less striking than many others. But the mystery surrounding the word/name Éarendel had been the focus of interest for many commentators throughout the previous century and further back. When I first came across the passage in Grimm, which quotes exactly the lines that Tolkien found so inspiring, I was tempted to think, and still do, that this might have been his starting point rather than the poem itself. My contention is that at this early stage in his academic career, Tolkien is likely to have used these kind of footnotes rather than referring to the original source material in the Icelandic Edda and the German book of heroes known as the Heldenbuch. There was no point in his reinventing the wheel when ready-made commentary was to hand. Not that it really matters, but it's worth noting that the lengthy account Tolkien gives of his discoveries is written fifty years later and may be subject to some rationalization. And when he discovered the intriguing name, he was not the venerable professor of later years – an image with which we are familiar because of his relatively late fame – but an ambitious twenty two year old undergraduate who thought he had stumbled across something new. It is a failing of the young to attribute originality to ideas they are discovering for the first time, but this is the way culture eternally renews itself, and in this case Tolkien's bright spark of inspiration ultimately led to the whole of his impressive literary achievement.

What does matter is that for at least a couple of years, Tolkien was pondering the mythological and linguistic provenance of the name. In a line famously quoted by Humphrey Carpenter and John Garth, when asked in December 1914 what the Gedling poem meant, Tolkien's replied, "I don't know – I'll have to find out".[11] That process of finding out took some time, and may have been in a relatively undeveloped stage when the first draft was written at Phoenix Farm. Christopher Tolkien writes interestingly in *The Book of Lost Tales Part Two* [12] of further attempts to fix the etymology of Eärendel in the context of his mythology. He tells us "...at the time of the earliest writing on the subject, the name was associated with the Elvish word 'ea' – 'eagle'". An earlier version of Eärendel's ship is called "Earame" or "eagle's wing". Perhaps here Tolkien was looking for a link with the Old English "earn" = "eagle". For the philologist, these

[11] *Tolkien and the Great War*, p.53 similar in *Biography*, p.102.

[12] *Book of Lost Tales Part Two*, p.266/7.

phonological links are just as important as the semantics in question and Tolkien, who had no ear for music, certainly had an ear for words. Nevertheless, it is puzzling that Tolkien does not make a link with the Old English "earn = eagle" just as he fails to mention Old English "ear = sea", as mentioned above. Perhaps in wanting to preserve the integrity of his own Elvish lexicon, he fought shy of complicating matters with traceable etymological links with Old English. In a letter to Milton Waldman,[13] he stresses his own Elvish meaning of Eärendil (sea lover) eager to dismiss the Old English and mythological roots of the word as "mere 'learned note'". Here he is concerned with his own fictional entity and does not want to become involved in some philological wild goose chase.

In the final analysis, the name Eärendel, or Eärendil, as it eventually became, is important as the name of a central character in Tolkien's developed mythology and fiction. Tolkien took care to sift the diverse ancient associations of the name to construct a new and coherent character, placing him in a key role in his invented mythology. The exact process of philological exploration that Tolkien undertook is largely a matter of speculation. Nevertheless, it points to the rich linguistic field that underpins his writing and suggests something of his meticulous methods of invention and discovery. What was a labour of love for Tolkien becomes a point of interest for his readers despite his clear caveats.

[13] *Letters*, p.150.

Chapter Seven

TOLKIEN'S SWISS HOLIDAY, 1911

The connection between Phoenix Farm and Tolkien's Swiss holiday of 1911 is slightly tenuous, yet it signals the beginning of the future close association of Jane Neave and the Brookes-Smith family and also provided Tolkien with material for episodes in *The Hobbit* and *The Lord of the Rings*. I am fortunate to have to hand Colin Brookes-Smith's typewritten memoir *Some Reminiscences of J.R.R. Tolkien* and I believe that this account sheds some new light on an episode, which is of interest to most Tolkien biographers.

In letters of 1961 and 1967, Tolkien reminisces about Switzerland. In the first letter,[1] to Joyce Reeves, he cites the expedition, as the source for an episode in *The Hobbit*, mentioning that the party was of a similar size. In the 1967 letter to Michael Tolkien,[2] he gives considerably more detail about the trip and makes particular mention of a hair-raising episode on the Aletsch glacier when the party was threatened by a falling boulder loosened by the sun. Of course, it is not only in the chapter entitled *Over Hill and Under Hill* in *The Hobbit*, but also in a similar experience in *The Ring Goes South* in *The Lord of the Rings* that he makes use of this material.

Colin Brookes-Smith's account is more of a sober itinerary, lacking the element of self-dramatization that we find in Tolkien's letter, but it is an interesting supplement and contains some revealing and entertaining material.

Holidays in Switzerland and the Austrian Tyrol were a regular fixture of life for the Brookes-Smiths in pre-war days, and they were accustomed to rope into their parties any friends and relations who were free to spend

---

1 *Letters*, p.309.

2 *Letters*, pp.391–3.

a few weeks tramping round the Alps. The party of 1911, shown in the photograph on page X, was made up of fourteen people.

The members were, from left to right, a Swiss guide, Helen Preston (a friend of Jane's from St Andrews), Dorothy Le Couteur (a school inspector), Mrs Muriel Hunt, Jeanne Swalen (a Swiss nanny), Ronald Tolkien (with white scarf), Hilary Tolkien (at back with white sweater), Jane Neave, a friend of Ronald's, not named, Rev. C. Hunt of Hurst Green, Phyllis Brookes-Smith, Colin Brookes-Smith, Tony Robson and Doris Brookes-Smith.

The journey from England took the party from Harwich to Ostende and thence by train to Cologne; the next stage of the journey was by riverboat to Frankfurt and from there by train to Munich and Innsbruck, which was to be the start of the "tramp". There had been some discussion about suitable headgear and clothing for the expedition, and the final choices were suitably eccentric and English. Two styles of tropical solar topee pith helmets were chosen, wide brimmed ones to protect the women's complexions from the sun, while the men wore the helmet versions. The ladies all had short skirts, which Colin believes caused some scandal because of the show of "legs". Each member was also equipped with an Austrian loden cloak and a spiked alpenstock. Finally, everyone wore hobnailed boots which Colin observes were practical but noisy, once causing a commotion when the whole party clattered into Innsbruck cathedral.

The party went by train from Innsbruck to the Rhone Valley and the Grimsel Pass. From there, a long dusty walk took them to Brig. Here Colin's account differs slightly from Tolkien's, who suggests that the party were very much roughing it. Colin says that the party rarely failed to find accommodation and he only remembers one night spent in a barn with the men on a haystack and the women down below. But sometimes, to accommodate a party of this size, hotels had to improvise. On one such occasion, when Colin, the Tolkien brothers and Tony Robson were sharing a bedroom, Ronald discovered an original way of teasing the German-speaking maid. When she enquired whether there was anything they wanted, Ronald replied "in a fluent gibberish with a guttural tang that sounded like German but was in fact nonsense". The maid exploded with laughter. They rang the bell again and the same routine was repeated.

Colin perceptively reflects how this "flair for imitating sounds that mimicked true language" was exploited in his later fiction. The episode also asks us to consider how firm Tolkien's grasp, at least of spoken German might have been. The other boys looked up to Ronald, as the oldest of the boys, and enjoyed his "quips and sayings". One he remembers was "Hannibal crossing the Alps with one eye and a mackintosh".

Following Dorothy Le Couteur's map of the tour, Colin goes on to mention an itinerary which includes, in this order, Visp, St Niklaus, Gruben, the Forcletta Pass, Grimenz, Hauderes and finally Arolla.

Arolla, which was the base for the final part of the holiday, was the location of several adventurous incidents. It seems to me likely that the material Tolkien used in his later fiction is probably very much an amalgam of these incidents.

On one day, the intrepid party climbed for a day over long scree slopes and finally over rock and snow to an altitude of 11,000 feet. Considering the presence of one small boy and several middle aged ladies, none of whom knew a thing about rock climbing, this was a daring venture. They were all roped together as they crossed the crevasses of the glacier. Colin remembers the sparsely furnished hut at the top of the climb, and particularly the "loo", which consisted of a gap between two rocks over a 1000 foot drop. With his typical gentle humour, Colin describes it as "highly" hygienic. It is the journey back to Arolla that Tolkien and Colin remember as the most hazardous. Rocks and boulders dislodged by the heat of the midday sun "came on in leaps and bounds making an unpleasant buzzing sound from rapid rotation. Some of the members of our party, particularly Dorothy Le Couteur had narrow escapes from these venomous and unwelcome visitors".

Colin's final memory is of a walk which ended in the party skirting a mountain by a very narrow path with towering rock on one side and an "apparently bottomless" valley on the other. At various points, the party had to negotiate protruding obstacles and Ronald took it upon himself to make fun of two elderly ladies whose fear was apparent by mimicking in his actions the exaggerated care they were taking, much to the amusement of the rest of the party. Tolkien seems to have been in high spirits on this trip, and the picture of him in the party shows him striking a humorous pose.

Colin's account reflects a high spirited fun-loving nineteen year old Tolkien but he also has something to say about Jane Neave. "It was Mrs

Neave who efficiently organised the commissariat and we always had good picnic food and tea made on methylated spirit stoves with tablet tea". The words Colin chooses reflect something of Jane's intimidating efficiency and leadership qualities and this, combined with her appearance in the photograph and her role organizing a party of thirteen other more Hobbit-like individuals, brings us back to the Gandalf theory. I am tempted to think that this image of Jane Neave with her wide-brimmed hat and staff, or a similar one published in the *Tolkien Family Album*, has caused undue speculation simply because it is one of the few, or perhaps the only one, so far published. More convincing perhaps is the evidence of her personality and appearance found elsewhere in this book. She was certainly tall, learned, mystically inclined, single-minded and not without a decided sense of humour. Perhaps we can forget the hat, the cloak and the staff, trimmings which may have their origin in a postcard [3] of an Alpine spirit, "Der Berggeist" Tolkien picked up before his return and wrote on the reverse side at a much later date "Gandalf?" Jane-as-Gandalf may be a largely fanciful idea, but it is an entertaining one and I can think of many more tenuous theories concerning real-life models in literature. If it is interesting or enlightening in some way to the reader and does not obviously distort the writer's intention, then all well and good. One final piece of evidence: according to his grandson, Richard Paxman, Colin Brookes-Smith thought that the character of Gandalf was modelled on Jane Neave. Colin only read *The Lord of the Rings* later in life and was no particular Tolkien fan, but when he came to the passage in *The Ring Goes South* which is modelled on the hair-raising Swiss adventure, he immediately saw Jane as the prototype for Gandalf. Coming from someone who knew Jane so well for such a long period, and who had no particular axe to grind in the field of Tolkien studies, this endorsement of the theory has to carry some weight.

J.R.R. Tolkien always preferred fictional to real-life adventures, and it is easy to see how the Swiss trip, with its sometimes risky incidents, furnished him with vivid memories that later brought fictional mountain adventures to life. It was probably also an episode that served to cement his relationship with Jane Neave, and it is in the 1961 letter in praise of "maiden aunts" that he recalls vivid memories of the Swiss holiday.

---

[3] *Biography*, p.59.

MAPS

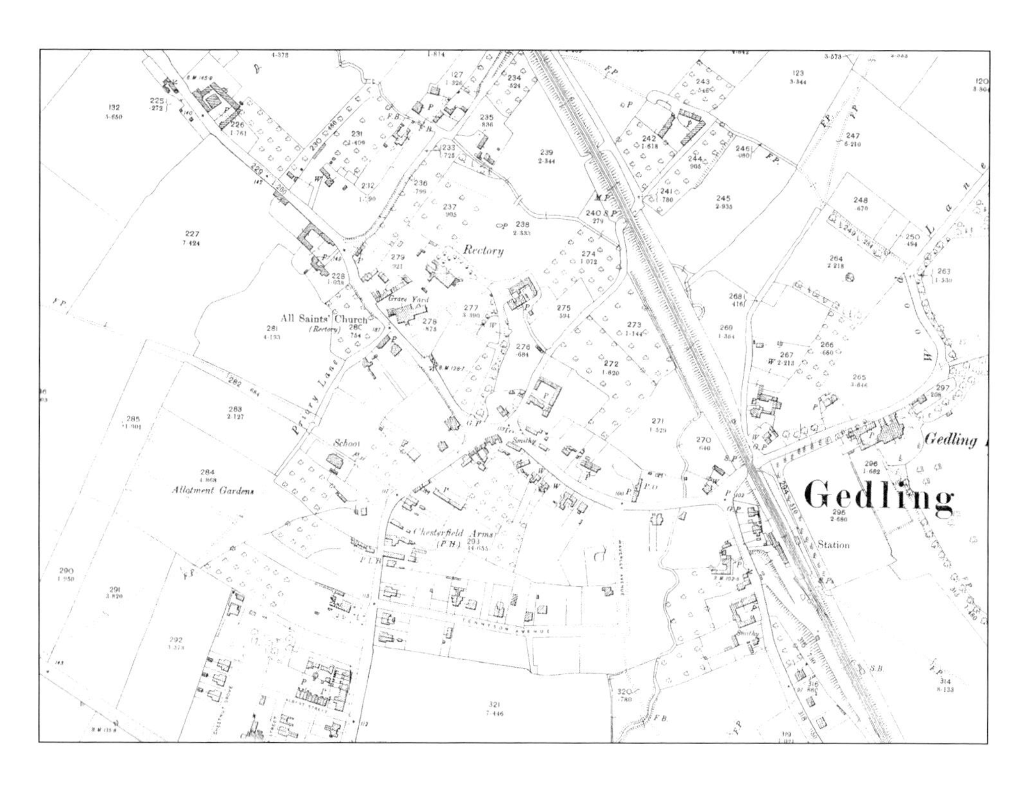

Based on the Ordnance Survey map of 1900, this map shows Phoenix Farm and Manor Farm towards the top left hand side. The extensive farm buildings and orchards can also be clearly seen. The limited extent of new building is also clear. "The Cottage", where Jane and Edwin Neave lived must be one of the handful of buildings close to the station on the east side of Shearing Hill and the "land and tenements" description might fit one of those below the station.

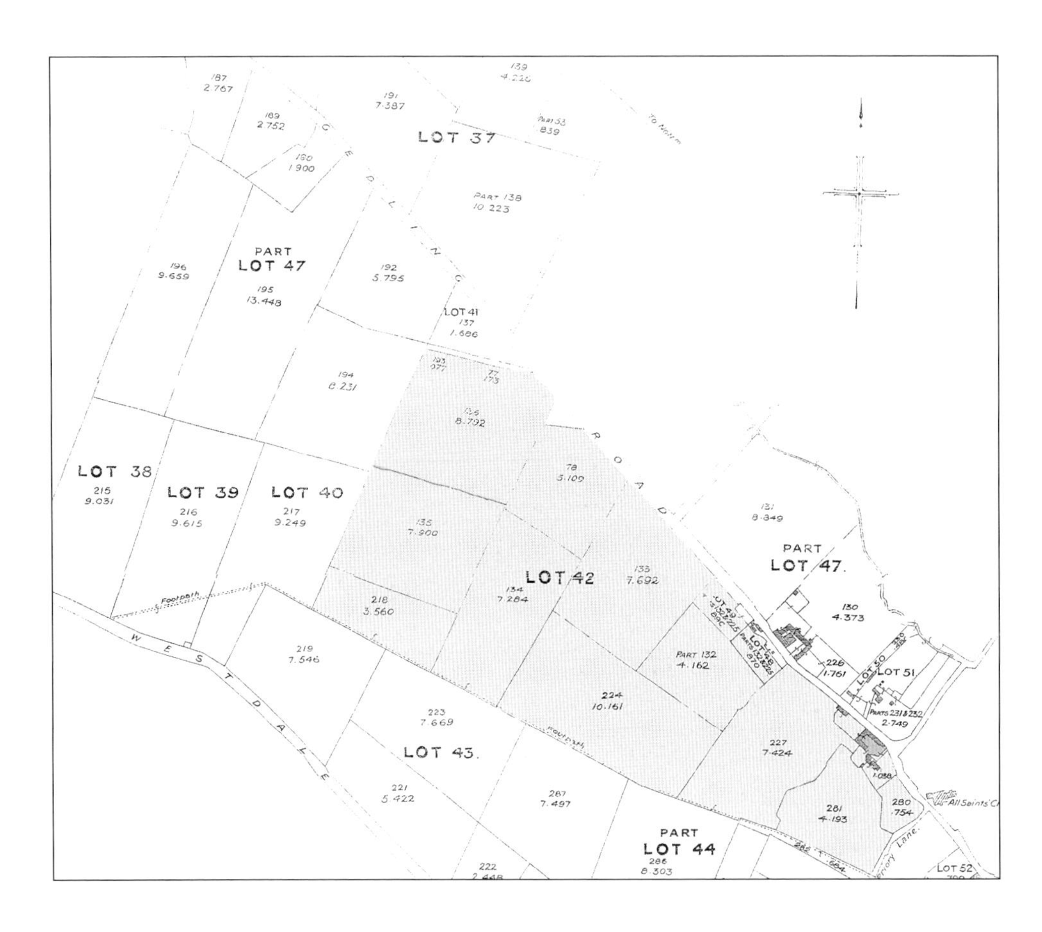

This map is taken from the original auction documents for the farms. The darker areas show Phoenix Farm and the lighter Manor Farm. The ridge between Westdale Lane and Arnold Land is marked by the very old footpath, now partly a made-up road.

RECOMMENDED READING

For a detailed account of the origins of the Eärendil stories and the poem *The Voyage of Eärendel the Evening Star*, Christopher Tolkien's account in *The Book of Lost Tales Part Two* is the best source. Tolkien's Letters are also dotted with references to the name and its significance, and here, of course, you can read a full account of what the author has to say on the subject. John Garth's interesting, very readable *Tolkien and the Great War* gives a fascinating account of Tolkien's life and writing at this time, particularly to do with the author's psychological state. With regard to Tolkien's state of mind, Wayne Hammond and Christina Scull's excellent *J.R.R. Tolkien, Artist and Illustrator* gives valuable insights. It also contains Tolkien's drawing of Phoenix Farm, which, before this publication, was the only published visual record of the place. Christina Scull and Wayne Hammond's *The J.R.R. Tolkien Companion and Guide* is a fascinating and wide-ranging attempt to order things Tolkienian in an encyclopaedic form; it is by far the best general reference book on Tolkien, both scholarly and readable (although not in one sitting!) Humphrey Carpenter's *J.R.R. Tolkien: a Biography* is still the best short biography of J.R.R. Tolkien. It takes a broad sweep at an awful lot of material and is still immensely readable.

For those interested in looking further into the name and figure of Eärendel, I would recommend Giorgio de Santillana and Hertha von Dechend's highly eccentric but fascinating work on "archeo-astrology" entitled *Hamlet's Mill: an Essay on Myth and the Frame of Time*. Originally published by Godine in 1977, the whole of the text is now published on the internet. (Eärendel is also the original name of Hamlet's father, but that, as they say, is another story). Carl Hostetter's article in Mythlore 1991 *Over Middle Earth Sent Unto Men* is an exhaustive account of the philological origins of Eärendel myth. I have not cited it in my bibliography because it only came to my attention after the writing of *Tolkien's Gedling*.

Books

Bibliotek der Angelsachsischen Poesie – ed. Grein and Wulcker Volume Three – 1896 Edition.

Crist – ed. Israel Gollancz – 1892.

The Exeter Book – ed. Benjamin Thorpe 1842.

The Blickling Homilies – ed. Richard Morris 1883.

Anglo Saxon Poetry – translated and edited by S.A.J. Bradley – Everyman.

An Anglo-Saxon Dictionary – Bosworth and Toller – Internet facsimile.

Teutonic Mythology Volume One – Jacob Grimm – Dover Publications.

The Letters of J.R.R. Tolkien – ed. Humphrey Carpenter and Christopher Tolkien – Harper Collins.

J.R.R. Tolkien: A Biography – Humphrey Carpenter – Allen and Unwin.

Tolkien and the Great War – John Garth – Harper Collins.

J.R.R. Tolkien, Author of the Century – Tom Shippey – Harper Collins.

The Lord of the Rings – J.R.R. Tolkien – Allen and Unwin.

The Hobbit – J.R.R. Tolkien – Unwin Books.

The Silmarillion – J.R.R. Tolkien – Unwin Paperbacks.

The Book of Lost Tales Part Two – J.R.R. Tolkien, ed. Christopher Tolkien – Harper Collins.

The Monster and the Critics and other Essays – J.R.R. Tolkien – Harper Collins.

J.R.R. Tolkien Artist and Illustrator – Wayne Hammond and Christina Scull – Harper Collins.

The J.R.R. Tolkien Companion and Guide – Christina Scull and Wayne Hammond – Harper Collins.

Memoirs

Ladies who Farmed In Gedling (unpublished) – Colin Brookes-Smith – 1979.

Some Reminiscences of J.R.R. Tolkien (unpublished) – Colin Brookes-Smith – 1982.

Archives

Nottingham University Manuscripts – Manvers Collection.
Nottingham University East Midlands Collection.
Nottinghamshire County Library.
Nottinghamshire County Archives.
St Andrew University Special Collections Department.
Birmingham University Archive.
King Edward's Foundation Archives.

Photographs

All photographs from the memoirs of Colin Brookes-Smith by kind permission of Jennifer Paxman. The pictures of Phoenix Farm and All Hallows Church, the front elevation of Phoenix Farm and the 1954 picture of Phoenix Farm looking up Arnold Lane, belong to All Hallows Church. The photograph taken from the All Hallows Bell Tower in 1954 is reproduced by kind permission of Robert Atkins. The 1908 picture taken from the church tower is by Henry Whittlesey of Netherfield, and belongs to the Bell Ringers at All Hallows Church. The picture of Gedling Colliery in 1910 is of unknown provenance, but the authors would be glad to include an acknowledgment in future editions. Photograph of the author by Norman Brown.

INDEX